Better Together

by

Nicholas Rose

Acknowledgements

I would like to thank Caro Handley, Professor Ernesto Spinelli, Cheryl Keen, Martin Weaver, Renato, Laura, Scott, Phil, Ola, Fairlie, Bruce, Kerry, Karen and all the people who have entrusted me with their concerns over the years, without whom this book would not have been possible.

Reading This Book

How do you want to read this book?

When you are faced with a concern in life, perhaps you are someone who tends to ponder and reflect, allowing your mind to wander through your differing experiences, feelings, and thoughts? Maybe you prefer to head straight into dialogue with others to see what happens if you explore a concern together, sharing experiences, and seeing how others think, feel, and experience? Or it might be that you tend to wonder about what resources already exist and like to find tools and techniques that other people have found useful?

Your approach to this book will depend upon your answers to those questions, and it will also depend upon your context. Are you in the middle of a conflict where you feel under pressure to find a resolution, or is there more of an exploratory quality to your interest? How much time and energy do you have? Do you want to dwell on a point, or do you need a quick steer?

In writing this book I have had the time to structure it in a way that makes sense of my own concerns with living. I tend to reflect on why something matters to me and I look to my own experience before I turn to that of others. It is then that I like to construct frameworks so that, when faced with new situations, I have tools and techniques upon which to draw. So, depending upon your answers to my previous questions, you might want to ponder and dwell, starting at the beginning and moving slowly through each chapter, or skim-read some chapters while saving focus and energy for others. Alternatively, you might want to go straight to a specific chapter. With that in mind, let me outline the structure of the book.

In the Foreword and Introduction I share why I've wanted to work as a relationship therapist and why I have written a book about that now. Chapters one to four are about the concepts, philosophies, language, and words that help me to think about relationships; thinking that directs my work as a relationship therapist. I write about how we experience relationships, how they form, where and when trouble arises, and how conflict can be addressed. So, that part of the book is for pondering and reflecting.

Next is a section that presents twelve stories to bring relationships and their dilemmas to life. While the characters are fictitious, the stories are built around my encounters as a therapist. If you prefer to read about how things actually work for others in practice then this section may be of most interest to you.

Finally, chapter five provides direction, structure, tools, and techniques that offer you a way of thinking about your own relationships. The chapter includes a series of questions aimed at deepening your understanding of the dilemmas you face, so that change can be facilitated.

Now that I have talked about how you might read this book I have a question: are you going to read it as fits your usual style and pattern of behaviour? I wonder what might happen if you choose to approach it in a different way?

Foreword

*What if every hurt, every conflict is down to something we are
yet to understand about our relationships?*

I hadn't been able to say why I wanted to be a relationship
therapist until I said goodbye to the first couple who had come
to see me for therapy. After seeing them out I closed the door,
and on sitting back down I had a feeling of pure joy, followed a
moment later by tears. At first I felt confused, and then I
thought of my mum and grandmother, who never had the
chance to get beyond the misunderstandings and
disappointments in their relationship before my grandmother
died.

As a child I had listened to their exchanges and could feel
the desperation and despair in their efforts to show each other
how they were failing to be loving. I remember feeling helpless
and unhappy, seeing them in so much pain. Even then it was
obvious to me that they were simply striving to love each other
in their different ways, but I was, at that time, without position,
language, or skills to help them.

I now know that misunderstandings that arise from differing
ways of what I think of as 'striving' can be uncovered and
corrected; that appreciation can flourish and that relationships
—any relationships, but most specifically those romantic and
sexual relationships between two people—can be the biggest
source of support, so that the partners know they are better
together and the only obvious word they can think of to make
sense of that is *love*.

I have found it really is not about right and wrong, good and
bad, disorders, dysfunction, disability, or about being 'woke',
or religion, culture, class, privilege, occupation, money,
ethnicity, gender, or sexuality. Instead, every hurt for every
person can be healed, not by time, not by change, not by action,

rights or laws, but by *understanding* something not yet apparent.

We are all in the world in our own unique ways: no one life is like another, no one body is like another, no one's experience is the same as another's. While everyone looks for similarities and anomalies, what gets so easily dismissed is the fact of universal individuality. The only thing we all truly share is our individuality and yet individual ways of being are increasingly pathologised and psychologised, a paradox that raises the question: are those endeavours really in the service of those who suffer, after all? Acceptance of uniqueness and asking the question *what do you need?* is so much more compassionate than the rush for the application of a label followed by a treatment protocol.

For one person, an empty plate is a sign of pleasure and appreciation, while for another, it is a sign that the receiver thinks the portion was too small. For both, appreciation is a shared concern, but how it is done and understood so obviously differs. For one person, to speak loudly is a way of helping another to hear; for another, a loud voice can hurt. How tragic that war can be waged when underneath it all we just want the same thing? We need not fear that we are different; instead we should think about the differing ways in which we are striving.

When we understand how we are striving, how another is striving, and how the differences create a relationship with its own unique dynamic and striving, we have a way of thinking about the discomforting feelings and confusion driving, perpetuating, and escalating conflicts. I refer to this sense of the relationship dynamic as 'togethering'.

Togethering is the time, energy, quality of engagement and consensus that form the basis for how I think about relationships, and in subsequent chapters I hope to be able to share the ways in which this approach is helpful.

Being able to help always brings me that experience of tearful joy. I couldn't help my mum and my nan so now I dedicate this book to them and hope that what I learnt from them, and from all the people who have confided in me since, might help others to avoid the pain and heartache that they endured.

Introduction

Why This Book Now?

This book might never have happened if it were not for the COVID-19 pandemic and the year of lockdowns. Extra time, combined with a powerful desire to offer something, make full use of my time and distract myself from my feelings of helplessness and impotence, pushed me to try to put into words what has driven me to work as a relationships therapist and to share what I have learned.

Indeed, there was something about the pandemic; the change and uncertainty that I saw played out by those who came to see me for therapy—as well as in my own relationships, including the one with myself—that reminded me of why I had become a therapist. Returning to my own therapist for online sessions created a different experience that enabled me to revise past trauma. It would not, I am certain, have been possible to do so in the physical presence of my therapist, irrespective of her undoubtedly supreme level of skill, experience, and unending care and compassion. I was reminded, after so many years, just why therapy and my being a therapist have been so central to my own striving and being.

Over the past twenty years I have had the privilege of insight into the experiences of thousands of relationships. So many different concerns, ways of thinking about things, experiences, disasters, triumphs, and feelings, and yet what is always shared is the joy, pleasure, and contentment when relationships are working and the pain, frustration, and fear when they struggle.

Change is one of those aspects of living that never changes. Relationship customs and approaches have always been subject to change as societies, religions, traditions, and cultures have created a constant flux in patterns of behaviour. At the time of writing, the pandemic, politics, climate change, and technology, along with the focus on mental health and psychology, are all impacting the freedoms and rights we have, the way we interact with each other, and what is considered to be acceptable. So much change and uncertainty challenges our sense of security, generating anxiety and fear, which can impact relationships even more than the changes themselves.

We are constantly encouraged to scrutinise our relationships and how we engage with them, as we are subjected to the increasingly complex language of psychology, rapid technological changes in communications, the impacts of social media, and changing rights for acknowledging genders, sexualities, and family structures, as well as movements such as Black Lives Matter and #metoo. All of this means that we are exposed to a constant barrage of views, opinions, and idealised and romanticised notions of relationships, together with ever-evolving expectations that make us look back in horror at what once was, and at how unskillful or plain wrong our previous behaviours now seem. I have noticed a shift in mainstream entertainment whereby people offer fellow characters 'amazing' insights and provide each other with labels from an ever-increasing lexicon of psychological terms. It seems we are now all expected to be able to provide each other with sophisticated analyses and insights into our psychological strengths and weaknesses, irrespective of whether we want either to receive or to offer them.

The COVID-19 pandemic was often said to have brought out the hero or the villain in each of us, with some praised for doing the right thing and others scorned for doing wrong. Our media was filled with articles on the psychological impacts of the pandemic as well as its impact on our relationships, creating further momentum and space for interest in psychological behaviours.

I believe that what the pandemic actually did was to bring into sharper contrast people's individual ways of thinking and doing things and to heighten the polarities in the ways people responded to both external and internal pressures. There's no doubt that the increased anxiety so many people felt led to behaviours that were judged as good or bad and, in many instances, pathologised, creating concepts that helped to speed up the breakdown of many relationships. Such concepts led to an increase in fear and anxiety for those being judged and for those doing the judging, rather than recognising difference and empowering people to work together to find solutions.

I witnessed struggles in relationships that were often only worsened by the introduction of psychological terms such as *gaslighting, narcissism, power imbalance* and *toxic relationships*. Such terms are always seen as weaknesses or failings as opposed to manifestations of people's striving. I have observed that in many cases this has served only to apply pressure that is clearly counteractive to improving relationships, disempowering those involved, and driving them in desperation to look to experts for treatments.

Some couples found that the pandemic brought them closer. They shared beliefs about and attitudes towards what was happening, so that they were in tune with one another and enjoyed spending more time together. For others, the pandemic created division. In addition to practical pressures such as finances, job security, home schooling, and lack of living space, differences in beliefs and values were revealed and became a source of anxiety and conflict. For some, the pause imposed by restrictions and lockdowns was a surprisingly pleasant relief, while for others, the sense of lost possibility threatened to derail their lives as their plans and dreams started to unravel and lose focus.

Disagreement over something apparently simple for which there is no compromise—mask-wearing is a good example, since you either wore one or you didn't—meant that differing beliefs and values came into sharp focus and conflict and unhappiness often resulted. Thrown together by lockdowns and various individual circumstances, the everyday concerns of work, finances, children, and families, all took on heightened significance. Furthermore, disparate views on politics, the role of authorities, the place for charity and community, and nature and nurture, meant that the apparent importance of having and vocalising opinions took on a supercharged force.

In many ways, the pandemic pressed the fast-forward button in an age in which self-actualisation is viewed as paramount; in which pathologising—viewing others as medically or psychologically normal or abnormal—is commonplace and serves to heighten the tension between the twin evils of loneliness and fear of others. The middle ground, meantime, appears to give way to increasingly extreme polarisation.

People seem now to have a more sophisticated understanding of themselves, their motivations and behaviours, and those of others. For some, however, the rejection of 'pseudo-scientific liberalism' moves them further towards the tendency to witch-hunt, to blame, label, judge, and dismiss others, especially via social media. Our young people are learning to communicate through imagery, character limits, and augmented reality. Individual identity is defined by the groups and interests to which you subscribe and your popularity within those groups. The words *connection* and *disconnection* provide a continuum of possibility that brings relationships and technology so succinctly under the same umbrella.

So, while the issues with which we commonly grapple in relationships have mostly not changed—love, money, trust, communication, parenting, sexual issues, health problems, addictions, and work-related stress—we also now grapple with a maze of terms that can be applied to ourselves, our partners, and our relationships. They can give rise to all kinds of questions and feelings. Gaslighting, coercive control, personality disorders, ADHD (Attention Deficit Hyperactivity Disorder), OCD (Obsessive-Compulsive Disorder), ASD (Autism Spectrum Disorder), abuse—verbal, physical, psychological or sexual—racism, sexism, homophobia, ageism, and abuse of power are all now in common usage. As a result, many people are looking more closely at their relationships and at what they think is really going on in them, which is what leads many couples to consider therapy.

Sometimes, couples come because they want to be better together, sometimes because they want reassurance that they are, in fact, better together, and sometimes because they have decided that they are no longer better together, and they want to find the best way to end the relationship. Sometimes that ending might mean finding a way to be better together at a greater distance, rather than being closer.

The decision to come to therapy might be prompted by a crisis such as a bereavement, an affair, or a job loss, or it might be the result of what is felt to be a change in one or both partners and therefore in the relationship. What each crisis has in common, though, will be a dynamic, a lived experience that has tipped the balance of the relationship from tolerable to intolerable.

Every relationship will change over time. Sometimes, the two people in the relationship change in step with one another, while at other times it can feel as though one person has changed in ways that the other finds hard to understand or challenging to live with. It is easy for us, over time, to forget the reasons why we connected in the first place, to become enmeshed in our difficulties and problems, and even to wonder whether we did really ever connect. Did we just imagine it?

To further complicate things, the parameters within which we used to measure our relationships have changed at great speed: partnerships and families are more diverse than they have ever been, with culture, gender, sexuality, and our ways of being together becoming more fluid. Similarly, language evolves at an ever-increasing speed, and we are called upon to learn new terms, because the use of those terms is taken up by many to offer a guide of character. Moreover, the correct use of language often seems to have greater import than the intentionality behind its use. Today, the choice we have of different roles is both an amazing achievement and a source of hope for many, but it is also a source of concern, insecurity, and confusion for many others.

Our societies have always adapted to the pressures of their times through the adoption of structures that are, for some, a source of liberation and opportunity, but oppressive to others. Every generation looks back at those who came before with horror and amazement at the ways things worked, what was acceptable then, and how much pain and hurt was inflicted and endured. So, it is not surprising that there always exists a background force that leads us to question the ways in which we strive and are togethering.

It is not unusual for a couple to arrive in the consulting room with one partner insisting that the other is gaslighting them, or is suffering from narcissistic disorder, is autistic, is unboundaried, or an alcoholic. Such familiar terms are widely used and often misused. All terms have the potential to help us understand things better and to find new ways of doing and being. However, psychological language is increasingly weaponised and inherently carries negative perceptions. With psychology now placed within the same sphere as medicine, any diagnosis brings a perception of sickness and the need for treatment to ensure recovery. And the diagnosable terms just keep coming, despite the fundamental matter of nature and nurture rarely being considered.

It's worth noting that any type of behaviour can be labeled as psychological when in reality an infection or purely physical phenomenon is at play. Here, I can think of a fairly extreme but very clear example: a story I read recently about a young woman who loved cooking and who was wrongly diagnosed with eating disorders, sectioned, and force-fed before being diagnosed with a rare medical condition. When I think of what she went through it sounds like torture, and I cannot bear the feelings such a thought arouses in me, so I must move along.

It seems we are mostly interested in terms that highlight weakness, inability, issues, and disorder—ones that can conveniently enable us to see other people as the problem and allow us to devote our time and energy elsewhere. In doing so, we miss the opportunity to see how we can be better at connecting, appreciating, and supporting our partners and better at building and sustaining our relationships. At a time when so many people talk about the stigma of mental health, there appears to be an equally forceful rush to apply terminology that perhaps reduces possibility rather than creating opportunity. Terms appear to classify people with a fixed set of attributes— narcissist, gaslighter, sociopath, psychopath—and to imply imperfection and unsuitability in the context of relationships.

I am not saying that everything is broken; a correct diagnosis can bring relief, resources, care, and treatments that return people to wellbeing. But even then, it can seem that wellbeing is something demanded of us by society as opposed to something that we can be left to individually strive for. What I am saying is that too often pressure—due to a lack of resources, time or energy, for example—can lead to a position being taken that is ultimately unhelpful. So often I have seen interventions that, on reflection, would appear to have enabled those around the sufferer to feel better as they wield their opinions, treatments and judgments, while the sufferer's experience is worsened by increased isolation and alienation.

I hope that this book will provide the reader with the insight, guidance, and encouragement to look behind the labels that we pin on one another and the judgments we make, to better understand one another, to feel safer and more confident with others, and to be able to appreciate and support others while receiving understanding, appreciation, and support.

However we are in any one moment of time is our way of being, our way of living, and the manifestation of our striving. If we start from that premise, we can take a step back and appreciate that simple state of being before we bring in our judgments, interpretations, and interventions.

I suggest that understanding each other's ways of being, doing and striving, and the relationship that two people have created together, provides a structure for moving forward. I want to show, through this book, how I have witnessed this approach working in relationship therapy.

I see therapy as providing a time and a space in which attention is focused on whatever is being expressed. It is about going back to the facts of the presenting issue, to see what is actually there, the way in which it is understood, and the responses to it. Therapy is about understanding our individual ways of making meaning, and only when our meanings are understood and appreciated can conflict be resolved.

This book is about just three things: you, the person you care about, and the relationship the two of you have created. I see the relationship itself as an entity separate from the two individuals within it. In any relationship there is *you*, there is *me,* and there is *us* and the unique dynamic that we have created. The relationship is the way *you* and *I* combined, and for me this vital distinction allows us to look at what is happening within a relationship without necessitating any blame for the partners.

I hope that you will feel encouraged to look at things from different perspectives, to find inspiration, to ask questions, and in so doing to realise that in relationships change comes about not by identifying what is wrong, but by recognising how misunderstandings and disappointments emerge. A conflict signifies something not yet understood, as partners strive to create and maintain a relationship.

It is my hope that what you read here will hold you, the reader, in a time and space of contemplation and reflection about life, the way we live it and how we understand others—especially those others to whom we feel closest.

It is my belief—and the premise of this book—that in order to be better together in our relationships we need to understand, appreciate, and support our selves, our partners, and our relationships in the best ways possible. In life, we only tend to question why we do things, or why our partners do things, when things happen that unbalance or disturb us. If we return instead to the idea that we are continually striving, and if we can understand what it is that we are striving for, and the way in which that is manifested then we have a way to keep track and think about what is needed, so that we are better together in our relationships.

Chapter One

Relationships and Togethering

Our relationships with partners can bring out the best and the worst in us and in others. They can give moments where the word *heaven* might come to mind and others that feel closer to hell. A relationship might offer a strong sense of identity, of who we are, or it might make us feel lost and dissembled. We can long for them, we can't avoid them, and we have to find our own way in them, not once but over and over again.

Relationships are also active and vital, constantly changing and moving. There's a word that, for me, is valuable in considering relationships, and that is *togethering*. I add the 'ing' to *together* because what I'm talking about here is a dynamic process, something that we are actively engaged in when we have a relationship with another person. I will return to this concept in the next chapter.

We are different in each of our relationships. We each have our own way of being, which will change depending on whom we are with. I might be more outgoing with one friend than with another, more anxious to please with a parent than I am with a child. We adapt to and alter in each relationship we have, and that is as true of romantic and sexual relationships as it is of any other. Often, the way we were with one another when we first met will set the scene for the 'us' that is our relationship.

In a relationship, every day brings the possibility that some new obstacle or event might prove unmanageable. We experience a constant tension in our relationships, always somewhere on a continuum of togetherness and separation. Much of the time we are somewhere in the middle but sometimes, when we stray to the extreme ends, powerful emotions test our relationships and us. Such tests can be some of the most important we will ever face.

Sometimes, tension applies generally across a relationship or only surfaces around specific concerns: security, money, family, relaxation, health, planning, sex, and fulfilment are major concerns that can cause conflict or highlight contradictions for us individually. However, relationships have to incorporate the needs and wants of all participants and the complexity of such a requirement can sometimes threaten to overwhelm and exhaust even the most patient of people.

That's why, at some point, everyone in a relationship will ask, perhaps many times over, *Are we better being together*?

Relationships are among the main pillars in life that make up our being in the world. Other 'pillars' might include health, spirituality, interests, and whatever brings us a feeling of security. These five areas constitute our personal world and all of them can interact and impact one another. A happy relationship may provide security, support your health, or involve shared interests and spirituality. Even when we don't necessarily share interests or spirituality with our partners, our wellbeing in all areas depends on the quality of our relationships.

Relationships, as with all the other constituent parts of life, have the potential to thrill or horrify, invoking through our senses an experience of communion with another person, or one of absolute alienation. They can involve feelings so powerful that we are caught up in the interaction and left floundering, attempting to make sense of and understand what we have just experienced.

Communion is a word that I choose to use specifically because of its transcendental associations. In communion we can momentarily lose our sense of separateness, of being alone in the world, or cast out, experiencing instead a sense of being entwined, connected, and merged so that the rest of life and the world is consigned, for even the briefest moment, to somewhere outside of our awareness. We are within, we are separate, we are everything—we are nothing?

Alienation, meanwhile, shows how powerfully the 'other' might be experienced as 'alien' and separate. It's a word that expresses the feeling of being thrown back onto oneself and how our senses, in terms of our bodily senses, emotions and thoughts, might bring this 'other' so totally and utterly into our awareness.

There are moments in our lives when another person's glance, word, gesture or touch can sends shivers through our entire being: that shared smile with someone we fancy; that expression on our parent's face; the quiet seconds sitting next to someone on a park bench; the holding of another's hand on a hospital bed; or that moment before you give or receive bad news, kiss for the first time or feel the blow of your attacker. At that moment, there is nothing to be done: it is a moment of pure being and when it passes we are compelled to act, to draw closer to or move further away from that encounter and that person.

We may feel attraction or repulsion or we may feel both, devastatingly combined. We may feel love and safety or hatred and terror. Or what we feel may be on a continuum somewhere between love and hate, attraction and repulsion, safety and fear. Irrespective of how pleasurable or painful these feelings might be, an encounter with another person has cut through the sameness of the everyday and something has been revealed to us about how we are in the world, who we are and how we are with others. What is going on for us? What has caused us to feel the way we do? The feelings we have are a call to action—how will we respond?

What I am describing, in these powerful momentary encounters and in our response to them, encapsulates what it is that brings meaning to our being in the world with others. And while we may have only a handful of such intense moments in a lifetime we are, throughout our lives, inextricably connected to other people, because relationships are an integral, essential, and defining aspect of what it is to be human. We couldn't and wouldn't exist without relationships; they are a timeless universal experience and a conundrum that we all share.

I use the word *conundrum* because we can never be entirely certain whether what we felt was fully shared and understood by the other person. We can believe it to be so, and we can hope or fear that it was, but ultimately it may be one of life's questions to which an answer may never be revealed. Communion is only ever an experience that we can agree might be possible and that, again, brings us back to its spiritual nature.

The type, quality and quantity of our relationships can range from casual to intimate, briefly fleeting to lifelong, deeply satisfying to troubling, and very few to many. Five seconds with one person can provide us with as strong a memory as a year spent with another. Hopefully, our experiences of communion will bring us relationships that nourish, sustain, support, protect, and strengthen us, and even bring an overall sense of peace and calm. All too often, however, relationships can lead to conflict, exhaustion, depletion, and disturbance.

As human beings we share the desire for communion with others—family, friends, partners—and the longing to feel loved and cared for. We long to know what it is to feel understood, to appreciate the closeness that comes with warm familiarity, or the joy of meeting someone we love whom we haven't seen for a long time. We long, too, with equal fervour, to be able to love and care for others and to reach the full potential of our capacity for love.

The experiences we have when we encounter others unleash a whole range of feelings in us—feelings that are universal. We know the force of the negative emotions—anger, fear, anxiety, and sadness—that can surface when we are hurt or under threat, just as we know joy, contentment, shared laughter, and love.

Connecting with others is core to our being. When we meet another person and we react with excitement, pleasure, annoyance, confusion, or dislike, it is because it matters to us. The way in which it matters will be uniquely personal, but it does matter. Have you ever met someone and had no reaction at all?

Might it be the fact of how we come to be that makes this inevitable? After a process of the division and multiplication of cells we are ejected or escape from our mothers' bodies so that, having been so deeply held and connected and physically attached, we are suddenly separate. From then on, we have a different experience of living; while still surrounded and interrelated there is also separation and disconnection. This formative moment happens at a time when we have no language to give shape to or contain our recollections, but our bodies always remember and they hold a truth around how we have known a way of being joined with another and being inside and a part of another. Maybe this is why, when it comes to relationships, there can be a yearning that is impossible to put into words—do we long to get back to, or wish to keep away from, that which we experienced before we had expression?

Does our desire for understanding with another person come about because we clearly experience our separateness, while our psychic interconnectedness is far less apparent? Science cannot yet explain all this to us and so, in the meantime, we are driven, guided, and informed by our experiences, by our hopes, and by humanity's jointly held notions of love and harmony. We are left to try to do our best, be our best, and hope to find those relationships where we have the greatest possibility of claiming the prized word, *love*.

For me, these questions reveal possibilities and highlight the unknowns of existence that we all share. Surely contemplation of the unknown has the power to create a moment of time and space in which compassion can flourish, even when faced by the most challenging of relationships? Yes, we are finding being with another difficult, but does the extent of this difficulty signify the extent of the pain?

It is through our relationships with others—parents, siblings, grandparents, friends, teachers, employers, colleagues, and, of course, our partners—that we know ourselves. What they tell us about ourselves, and the way we observe ourselves with them, helps us to form our sense of self and of who and how we are.

We gather information and feedback from our relationships all the time. Someone we are related to, or in a relationship with, may say something or express something that connects or resonates with us. Or we might feel or think something in relation to them that makes sense to us. We also use relationships for comparison and to inform us about new people in our lives. For instance, a new person might remind us of someone important to us. We might think, *They are like Alex, who meant a lot to me, so I think I will like them.* Or, *I need to*

be careful here, Dani hurt me and so I feel wary with this person.
Relationships with others remind us of the way we are as well as of the way we are *not*, and we look to our relationships for confirmation, reassurance, and safety, although this is not always what we get. Our relationships form a system in which we are located and who we are, the way we are, and the way we feel and think come from that place.

When we meet someone new it is this unique experience of our own personal relationship system that will bring meaning to the encounter. There might be excitement, anxiety, curiosity or fear, but what is certain is that connecting with a new person is an encounter to which we will bring all that we have known and become up to that moment, yet free of the experiences, judgments, and interpretations borne of time spent together. It is therefore no surprise that the initial encounter will shape the rest of the relationship.

In first meetings, the joy or comfort that comes from somebody saying something that connects with us and that is experienced in a truthful and authentic way can be either a wonderfully affirming experience or leave us shaken and off balance. Feelings lead us to jump to conclusions and make hasty judgments; when we are in pain it is natural for us to want to locate its source and find a resolution and when there is ecstasy it is natural for us to find its source and replicate it.

In our relationships the psychological pain we suffer can be eased by developing a position that makes sense of it, most likely through attributing it to something that someone said or did, which creates a conflict in us and is therefore a threat to our 'system'. The area in our brains that is responsible for this is called the amygdala. For our amygdala there is no right or wrong, good or bad; there is only what is familiar and historically experienced—that which brings wellbeing or suffering—or what is unfamiliar and has to be processed so that it can be judged as potentially safe, neutral or harmful.

In relationships and the search for connection, we usually try to make sense of and understand what someone else says and the way they say it. We can tend to take what is said at face value, but whether a perceived criticism is hurtful or not depends to a great extent on what the intention of the speaker is, no matter whom they are. What is said to us and what we say is never simply about the words; the way we feel and the delivery of what is said is so important that we are always tuned into it. If it is someone who cares for you, and who feels kindness, compassion, and empathy then something that might be hard to hear can be said in a way that it is helpful. On the other hand, we might feel hurt or dismissed by a single comment or momentary facial expression.

It can be helpful, before interpreting something that is said to us as simply unkind, to look at the state of the person who has said it. Are they tired, stressed, irritated, unwell, under pressure or feeling upset? We put a huge emphasis on words, but what someone says is based on how they are at the moment when they speak, and what we say is so often not what we really mean. And, of course, the way they speak to you may be the way they speak to others and, crucially, to themselves. Do they use an internal critical narrative to guide their own life?

They may not be intending to sound unkind; they may simply be feeling the kind of 'dis-ease' that results from lack of kindness or self-care in their life, or they may be trying to help you in a way they believe is helpful. It can also be helpful to consider our own state when we experienced that interaction – did we go into it tired, frustrated or irritated? What was in our awareness just before the encounter? When we think about what was said, and how, are we certain that at another time and in another mood we would have come away with the same view? Did we enter into the encounter in a state of ease? And are we open to the possibility that other people might just 'do' their thinking differently?

We may well make a judgment based on our experience of the words used and the tone of voice or demeanour of the person talking to us, but there will be so much that we cannot know, especially if we don't ask.

We, of necessity, make judgments all the time in order to navigate life and give it meaning. To be conscious is to judge: am I too hot or too cold? Do I cross the road here or there? Am I on time for work? To judge is not wrong; it's a necessary part of life. We use judgment to keep ourselves safe and it illuminates for us areas for our attention. But judgments are not truths, nor instructions or rights or laws, they are simply conclusions that can lead us to actions that are either skillful or unskillful.

There is a human tendency to try to locate causes. It is a natural learning process. If we put a hand on a hot pan not realising it was hot, we burn ourselves. We learn, therefore, that we should be careful around hot pans before touching them, and we internalise the judgment that it is a mistake to touch a hot pan.

But have you noticed how, when someone has learnt a painful lesson, they often tend to judge themselves for choices made before the experience? Saying things like, 'I was so stupid to touch that hot pan'. So often our initial feelings of pain and hurt are replaced by feelings connected with embarrassment or shame, for having been someone who could experience pain and hurt.

Aren't we all trying to be as safe as we can be and the best that we can be? If so, doesn't that explain why, when things go wrong and we can't control events or do things in the way we believe to be for the best, we use judgment to reject what we don't like or what scares us? And we are always under pressure, as we navigate our way through myriad situations, decisions, and interactions every day.

Take for example social media, where judgment and opinion expressed in just a few words is the norm. The danger here is not only the speed of response, but also the fact that people are judging based solely on what is shown, without actually experiencing the person on the other end of a tweet or an Instagram picture. When something has been put in front of us by someone else it is natural for us, through our need to be safe and the best that we can be, to judge. Sometimes, however, we don't even realise that we are making a judgment: it is ingrained into our vocabulary or consciousness and has become so commonplace that we don't recognise it. For example, when you hear someone described as 'hysterical', what gendered person are you expecting? Likewise, the gender associated with the term 'anally retentive'?

To take another example, judgment can be made on the basis of how many friends someone has. If they have 10,000 friends on Facebook, one might ask, 'Yes, but do they have any *real* friends?' Or, if that person has ten friends, they might be judged as 'sad' because 'nobody likes them'.

Negative judgments can also be used as a form of self-comparison, something along the lines of *I should have more friends*, thereby creating tension about where we are on a continuum of 'okay' to 'not okay'. I like to think about this in terms of the anxiety that uncertainty can generate. Questions demand answers, they nag away at us, distract us, and take away our energy, so it is not surprising that instead of questioning our judgments, we often prefer to take a position and, in this way, move on to something else. Again, our propensity for doing so can be thought of in terms of a position on a continuum, with some people questioning even their questioning, while others declare their truths as universal truths.

Many of us are affected, to a greater or lesser extent, by the labels our parents have given us, in some cases based on judgments they made about us when we were very young. We can reach adulthood thinking of ourselves as shy, or outgoing, funny or clever, slow or quick-thinking, anxious, extrovert, sporty, bookwormish, and so on.

Labels tend to restrict and cage us; they can so easily tip from being something helpful and liberating to being oppressive and painful. And for the one applying the label, what is their intention? Are they certain they are being helpful, or are they simply alleviating their anxiety around their role as parent? For example, in a restaurant I saw a child state a strong aversion to the smell of mint sauce. In response, the parent told the child they were just making a fuss and being difficult. I'm not sure why the parent responded in that way, but I wondered whether the parent was missing a possibility. Could it be that the child was revealing a uniqueness that, if understood, could set a course for the rest of his life? Could he be a world-leading perfumier in later life? Or could this sensory reaction have been an indication of an infection?

Take *introvert* and *extrovert*, which are terms very commonly used in families, but which are not necessarily useful. I have spoken to many people over the years who say that in some situations they might be extrovert and in others introvert; few people feel they are one or the other all of the time. I like to think of labels as snapshots in time that give us a direction for further study, because in life we are always becoming, always evolving, changing, and emerging. This is an indisputable fact: we are a collection of cells and science can show the constant death of cells and the creation of new ones.

Think about the word *happy* and see what comes to mind. Now imagine yourself doing this ten years ago—what would have come to mind then? Ten years on and the thoughts, images and feelings in your body will be different because you have more experiences of situations that have led you to feel happy and unhappy. Your relationship with happiness has changed. So even if people think of you as a happy person, it really does a very poor job of capturing you in any meaningful way.

This is true of relationships too. Our partnerships often attract a great deal of judgment from ourselves and from others. Is someone too old or young, too inexperienced, too self-absorbed, too ambitious or not ambitious enough? Too loud or quiet? The wrong culture? What matters most is the recognition of our judgments and the understanding that judgments are simply conclusions based on who we are, who we have been, what has happened to us, and the way we are at that moment in time. As we are constantly changing, so our judgments will change too—everything is in constant flux.

We all operate on continuums of pressure, which are not necessarily the same from one day to the next. On a day when I am feeling bright and full of energy, I might love your company and find it refreshing and energising. But on a day when I am tired, I might find you too loud and talkative and feel stressed. For you this might be confusing—are you too loud, or are you great company? Well, you are both, depending on how *I* am. And how might I come across to you? Am I dull one day, fun the next? Probably. Maybe if we can tolerate this as a universal, then it might be possible to avoid the exhausting and tumultuous experiences that come from constantly trying to locate problems or qualities in each other and in ourselves.

This is, in part, why relationships can sometimes be difficult and challenging and at other times satisfying and rewarding. Navigating our relationships with care and consideration, insight and understanding is a lifelong quest we all undertake. And this is never truer than when it comes to the relationship with our partners.

We are called upon to always reflect and try to find the answer. *Was it me? Was it you? Was it us?* The relationships that I experience as being the strongest are those where the couple are committed to exploring those questions together, seeing them as a joint project, as a responsibility that is part of being in a relationship together and as the mechanism for maintaining understanding, appreciation, support, and the possibility of that felt sense of 'communion'—a relationship that overall brings a sense of ease and peace.

When we first meet a potential partner there will inevitably be intensity in our disposition. We might strive for understanding—watching, listening, clarifying, feeling tentative, focused or interested. Or we might feel excitement, anxiety, desire or even uneasiness. And while, later in the relationship, our disposition doesn't change, the level of intensity we apply almost certainly will, so that we will not give the same focus to our interactions as we did when we first met. However, when we remember that this intensity of focus was our way into closeness initially, it can help support us in our attempts to return to the state experienced before disappointments, misunderstandings, and conflict appeared.

Chapter Two

Getting Together

The relationship we have with a partner will almost certainly be the most illuminating and complex of all our non-familial relationships. When we choose to navigate significant periods of our life side by side with another person, we undertake great challenges along with the capacity for great growth, both individually and together.

Until science can prove otherwise, it is reasonable to conclude that every relationship the world over is unique. No two are the same; everyone's experience in a relationship is unique because we all have our own way of being (striving, living) in the world, and that will create our approach to relationships. So, the universality of relationships is the individuality, and this assumption is the foundation, the bedrock, and the starting point from which to begin the process of understanding any relationship and any conflict.

Our feelings upon meeting another person will tell us if this is someone whom we wish to know better. And the strongest positive feelings alert us to the potential for our closest relationships.

As we move through life, events occur that challenge our hopes, dreams, and expectations. As a result, all kinds of feelings are generated and at times we are pulled into ourselves and a curtain is drawn around us, shutting out the outside world and those close to us. At such times, we can long for someone able to step inside the curtain to share our experience, and there is a collective human hope that this will be our partner, just as we would hope to be for them.

The story of any relationship always starts well before the partners meet for the first time. In the previous chapter, I talked about the relationship 'system' we each come from, which means that who you both are the moment you enter each other's life is vital. Your system will encompass what has happened to you, what are you hoping for, what has been achieved or is yet to be achieved, how important a relationship is for you at that point in time, your eagerness for a relationship, how you are feeling, what your priorities are, what relationships you have had, how you feel and think about relationships, the ones you currently have and what you hope for the future.

The way a partner comes into your life will also have significance for all that ensues between the two of you. Not just the way you meet (although this will be important), but the 'dance' between you as the relationship forms: the getting to know you stage, the 'firsts' that you share (the first date, first kiss and so on), and the emphasis that each of you places on every aspect of the relationship. The heightened emotional system that originates in our need for safety and survival means that what is significant about the experience of any first meeting for us always contains vital information about our understanding of the situation, the other person, the relationship, and ourselves. We will start to develop an understanding and expectations against which we will experience the relationship going forwards. And crucially, if there is any misunderstanding at this point, it will remain in the relationship until it is addressed.

The societal shift towards choice, freedom, migration, personal responsibility, and self-individualisation in an information age, means that the ways in which we find partners are unrecognisable compared to twenty years ago. Arranged marriages, introductions, family matchmaking, and local community have declined in importance, while dating apps, commercialised relationship psychology, and personal information have moved in. For example, maybe there are five thousand potential matches for you according to a dating app, so the app will narrow down your search, matching you by grouping you and others using labels such as 'love of nature'.

When you do meet, whoever makes the first move might be worth noting. Did you choose or were you chosen? Is this a pattern of behaviour for you or the other? What might have been different if that choice had been different?

When two people first feel drawn to one another and are in the process of forming a relationship, there is so much information contained in what happens and doesn't happen, what is spoken about and what isn't. Every moment, interaction, and activity is putting in place a pattern of behaviour and expectations, and through it all both partners start to develop their own understanding of what is happening.

In this way, there develops the belief and feeling that there's an understanding between you both. This is not necessarily explicitly spoken—it may well be implicit—but it forms the basis of the relationship; a kind of mutually understood agreement that you want to be together, and to be together in that particular way.

By that stage, the two of you have created a third entity—the relationship. For me this is fundamental; the relationship is the way you both act in relation to each other and the world. Once we are in a relationship with someone else, we can act, feel, and think differently to our individual selves, sometimes in very evident ways, sometimes in intangible ways. Sometimes we feel more relaxed, or happier; we might laugh more but we may also laugh less or worry more or less. For instance, perhaps you always pay your share of a meal, but with your partner you are happy to pay for both of you or to be treated to the meal by them. You might do something spontaneous, which would not be your usual style. Perhaps you like to drive everywhere, but with your partner you find that you suddenly feel like walking together. Or you might be creative or practical together in ways that you would not be otherwise. In this way, we are ourselves plus this other entity, the relationship.

The word *communion* resonates, as it is the core experience of being with another. It will be the foundation of the experiences and hopes and form the expectations around understanding, appreciation, and support in the partnership. Desire may or may not be present, important or constant. The biological components of sex mean that the presence or absence of sex does not define a relationship. However, the word *love* is one that, despite its purely felt, experienced, and spiritual connection, is almost always present. As with communion and other intrapsychic experiences, it is never possible to know whether something is truly shared. However, at times when we find ourselves hesitant or uncertain, an agreement with another that the word *love* feels right to use can provide the reassurance and encouragement needed to stay in the relationship or to make a change.

When something doesn't feel right about the use of the word *love*, it can result in great pain and frustration. Although seemingly relevant, the question *What is love?* is less important than the answer to the question *Do you both feel this is this a loving relationship?* Both partners need to be able to answer yes for the statement to be true.

When we are with another person, however close we are to them, feelings and thoughts will arise in us that we believe to be ours alone. In that moment, we have a binary experience of either being in communion or being separate or alienated. If we take a step back and think about the experience of being together over a period of time, then we can think of our experience of communion and alienation on a continuum.

If you are thinking about your relationships, perhaps the one you are in now, ones you had in the past, or the ones you wish to have in the future, they will all contain a number of moments when, for whatever reason, your otherness or sameness will come into vivid focus. Both experiences contain so much valuable information about you, your partners, and the relationship.

The point is that even when we know someone well, we don't always know what is going on underneath the surface. Our relationships are complex to navigate, and we need to stay open, ask questions, suspend judgment, and be prepared to accept that for someone else, even someone you are very close to, things might be different to the way they are for you. In fact, they almost certainly will be different. This is because what matters to us individually at any one moment in time is likely to be different, as is evidenced by the collection of witness statements after an incident. Every witness will have experienced the moment differently and will therefore provide a unique account. In my experience of relationship conflicts, the partners always hold differing truths. Most of the time the balance of the relationship means that this phenomenon is acceptable, but the balance can shift, such that the discrepancy threatens to bring into question our sanity.

At the same time that we are on a continuum of communion and alienation we are always somewhere on a second continuum of togetherness and separation, so that we experience a constant tension. This can be especially challenging in our romantic relationships. Right from the start there will be this tension about time and activities spent together or apart.

As couples navigate this continuum there are continual decisions to be made: how much time should we spend together? Do we see friends separately or together, or both? Should we have two date nights or one? Do we holiday together or apart? Do we travel separately and meet at the destination or travel together and spend less time together at the destination?

Some might choose to spend all their time together, which raises the question of how easily they are able to manage without one another, and the ultimate question of what they both think it would be like for the one left behind, when one dies. Another couple might be the proverbial ships that pass in the night, and that might work for them, which raises the question of how and whether the relationship will manage to support each of them when major life events occur, such as an illness or redundancy.

It is the tension around the time we are spending, or not spending, with a partner and our reaction to that state of affairs and decisions made around it, that keeps us in balance. What do I mean by balance? Let me give you an example. Suppose you feel in the mood to have pizza for supper but, when you suggest it to your partner, they say they recently had pizza and would prefer Chinese. After what feels for both like a frustrating amount of repetitive and pointless talking, the idea of Indian food somehow gets raised. This feels good for you, for your partner, and for the relationship. In agreeing to let something go (the pizza) you have gained something—a peaceful evening at home sharing food with your partner. The evening is what you really want, and for that to happen you don't need pizza. For your partner it may be the same; they can let go of the idea of Chinese food in order to have the evening together you both want. In this way you have balance.

There is another term I use that seems to express so clearly what I mean. *Epoche* is a Greek term meaning, roughly, 'suspension of judgment'. I think of it as a kind of letting go, not with a grumpy 'whatever', or even with a Gallic shrug of goodwill and acceptance; it is more a felt sense of shift where suddenly something solid becomes ethereal, or something ethereal becomes solid. Something is revealed to us, and we might say, 'It is what it is', or '*que sera, sera* [whatever will be, will be].' And through this experience of epoch we are able to move into a felt sense of ease, the tension no longer present and a sense of resolution. I use the word *ataraxy,* a word also of Greek origin in which the mind is tranquil and untroubled by worry, to convey a felt sense of things being as they should be.

Of course, much of the time we might just go along with what a partner wants, but at times when we need something different, resolution and *ataraxy* will only be possible through the partners working together to reach that moment of *epoche*. In my experience relationships only run into serious trouble when partners start to lose faith that achieving *epoche* and *ataraxy* is still possible.

Let me digress for a moment to explain a little more about those two terms. In reflecting on times when I have experienced *epoche*, I think of it in terms of a shift in my whole being. There is a physical aspect, a sense of a shift in energy, feelings that come when something is revealed, but before we decide whether what is revealed is good or bad. Images come to mind such as swimming underwater and heading for the surface: that moment when you move from being underwater to above water, or the moment when, walking in a forest, you come to a clearing. It's a complete shift in experience. Can you think of moments like that? The term *epoche* works for me as a way to describe it, but maybe there is another word that captures such an experience for you?

And then the word *ataraxy* makes sense for me in thinking about the experience that comes *after* such a moment. It conveys a feeling of calmness, or equanimity, a sense of relief or perhaps healing. Again, when I think of such moments I think of a change in my body, such as my shoulders relaxing, or the way my body feels straight after an amazing stretch. The image I have is of coming inside after being out in a storm; the feeling of having reached a calm place where it is possible to stop and just be. Thinking of your own experience, what word or words captures this experience for you? I use the terms *epoche* and *ataraxy* elsewhere in this book, so if they seem unfamiliar or unrepresentative to you, then do use your own words or images in their place.

In reflecting on where you and your partner are on the continuum of togetherness and separation, it can be useful to bring other relationships into this thinking. Our families, the ones we grew up in, influence our way of being in the world, whether we choose to continue their patterns or to do the opposite. For example, if one of you has a big family that is always partying together, you are likely to have different expectations to someone who comes from a family where everyone was perfectly happy spending most of their time in separate rooms.

In my experience, people often compare themselves to their parents and recognise similarities, but some of the most powerful moments in therapy have come when someone realises that maybe the fact they are not similar is actually a reaction against their parents' way of being. Their determination not to be like their parents means they are far from free.

Families certainly affect our choice of partner. While we can't choose the relatives we are born with, we believe that we can choose those we spend our adult life with. Without doubt the system of relationships we have in our early years has a bearing on the partnership choices we make later. It's almost inescapable that our experiences when younger will have an influence. So, to what degree are we choosing, as opposed to finding ourselves within comfortable parameters? Do we end up with, in other words, someone just like Mum, Dad or a sibling? And those who insist their partner is nothing like Mum or Dad might well find that their parents have still influenced the choice, only in the opposite direction.

We all enter into situations with others with intentionality; one that is intimately connected with our understanding of what is good and bad and what we should strive for to ensure our lives have meaning. That opinion is based upon self-awareness; the information we gather about ourselves, and what we learn about the world and those around us. What this means is that in every interaction with another person we are carrying a complex expectation of how we and the other person should be. And when this expectation is not met, we experience things as going badly and as conflict arising.

Of course, we know that in all relationships there will be misunderstanding, differences of opinion, and challenges brought about by events in our lives. All of that feels manageable while we believe we are with someone where communion is possible. It follows that when a relationship falters it is because it has become a place of misunderstanding and fear—in other words, of disturbance. And when this happens, we struggle to comprehend what it is we need to do to restore communion, to achieve *epoche* and experience *ataraxy*.

This is where I come back to *togethering*, the concept of actively 'doing' a relationship. Togethering is something I pay a lot of attention to when I work with partners, and I break it down into four components: Being, Doing, Engaging, and Agreeing. These are the areas that I look at closely. In what way are the partners matching one another? In what way are they dissonant with one another?

While the felt experiences of appreciation, support, and understanding matter and are almost always given as reasons for coming to therapy, the words themselves are so laden with judgment that their use can add to conflict. Partners end up arguing over who is the most and least appreciative, supportive or understanding, while the actual concerns, the ones that need discussion, are overlooked. For me, the components of togethering provide a more neutral framework for identifying the causes for the conflicts arising from the partners felt experiences around appreciation, support, and understanding.

Through these components it is possible to spot a gap, a mismatch, a misunderstanding. They tell us much about the way both people in a relationship are living and connecting.

There are no rights or wrongs regarding the aspects of togethering; the relationship's health can be understood in terms of how it is for the partners. Understanding this is possible through considering the level of satisfaction the partners have overall as well as in relation to the togethering aspects.

The first component is *Being*: the time spent together. Are those in the relationship happy with the amount of time they are spending together? It doesn't matter whether this is a lot or a little, as long as they both agree. For some partners, being together almost all the time is comfortable. Paul and Linda McCartney famously only ever spent one night apart during their thirty-year marriage, when he was arrested in Japan—and that, they said, was what they wanted. At the other end of the spectrum are those who spend long stretches of time apart. Perhaps their work takes them away from one another; perhaps they like to travel separately or even to live in separate homes. There is no right amount of time to be spending together. Difficulties only set in when one is happy with the time spent together and the other is not. If only one person is happy then it is not a happy relationship.

As a therapist I am sometimes alerted to the fact that time itself might be an issue when a couple struggle to find a time when they can both attend a session, want differing session lengths, frequency, number of sessions, or use sessions to organise future sessions. It might be that they struggle with the administrative aspects of being in a relationship.

The second thing I notice is what the two partners are *Doing*: how much energy have the two people got for each other? Some will have lots of energy to do things together, or perhaps to enjoy being together in a quieter, more restful way. Some people are active and busy outside the home, so home becomes a retreat, the place where they can unwind and be at ease. For others, home is an active and busy place, where they do a lot together.

If there is an energy mismatch, or something disturbs the energy, complications can arise. For instance, one person might suggest that their very active partner has ADHD (Attention Deficit Hyperactivity Disorder) while the other might suggest that their much quieter partner is depressed. What matters here is not the labels, which can be unhelpful, but the mismatch in energy.

The energy in a relationship can also be disturbed by external factors, such as health issues, the arrival of children, a demanding new job, and so on.

Of course, energy levels will fluctuate and change. Someone might become exhausted, and their energy level sags, and then something will shift and they will find more energy. Another person might have very high energy levels but find that this diminishes over time. What matters is the agreement between the couple that the energy each of them has—and their relationship has—is working for both of them.

The third component of togethering is *Engaging*, and this comprises both spoken and non-verbal communication. What a couple chooses to speak about and the way they talk to one another is key.

Some couples can argue a lot, which might at times alarm those around them, but it may be that they're not concerned about the fact that they are shouting at each other and they're quite happy with it. Others might be very quiet and hardly speak to each other at all. And this might work well for them.

In both cases, people can judge for themselves the way they are. Those who say, 'we never argue' are worried because they have read that the best relationships are the ones where there are some arguments. So, then they wonder if they should argue.

Partners who shout a lot might also worry that their way of doing things is wrong. But ultimately what matters is that they are happy with the number of arguments they have. There is no right or wrong in terms of how much argument takes place within a relationship.

The real question is how helpful the exchanges and the arguments are. You can have the same argument over and over and it doesn't resolve anything, or you can have a quiet conversation that resolves things. It might also be the other way around, as talking quietly may be filled with unresolved friction, and shouting might lead to resolution.

Talking can be a battleground. It's common for one person to say, 'she's too emotional and she talks to much' while the other says, 'he's too quiet and won't express his feelings'. But what is at issue here is not the language or the words used or the volume, or whether the language is emotive or cognitive. It's not about talking about feelings or facts—it's to what degree two people in a relationship strive to see each other, themselves, and the relationship they have created as they are, rather than as they want them to be or think they should be.

Non-verbal communication is just as important as the spoken word in the act of engagement. Eye contact, touch, silence, physical distance, facial expressions, bodily movements, noises, and posture all contain information about how we are, and the degree to which partners understand each other's non-verbal communication, is vital. In the same way, angry words can hide underlying feelings, as can angry gestures.

Often, partners in trouble can end up arguing about how to speak properly, demanding, 'You've got to talk to me, you've got to tell me how you're feeling, you never tell me, you expect me to read your mind . . .'

But of course, we do often have a good sense of what the other person is expressing, even when they are not explicitly saying it, but our own discomfort with how it sits with us means that it can be easier to ignore the communication. For example, if we are not hungry but we know the other person is, we might choose to ignore that, saying to ourselves something like, 'If they can't say they are hungry then that's not my fault'. My point is that if we've got the energy and the willingness, we will fill in the gaps and make allowances for the person who doesn't say how they feel, just as we might make allowances for the person who tells us all the time how they feel. So, in this instance, rather than saying, 'Just stop telling me how you feel, I'm fed-up with it,' you might say, 'Oh you're sad, what is it that's happened?'

If we are willing to pay full attention both to the verbal and non-verbal language of the other, if we can fully engage with them, then most of the time we will know what is going on with that person.

Sometimes, the verbal and non-verbal are out of step with each other. Someone might be quite defensive verbally but at the same time appear relaxed with their partner. Or they might be stomping around the house while speaking very calmly. It's useful to note that people tend to choose whichever form of communication suits them.

Engaging is about thinking and talking, and one of the things I find most significant in togethering is the degree to which two people are thinking and talking, either with one another or about one another.

When we spend more time thinking or talking about the other, rather than together, then togethering can be out of balance. It can sometimes feel easier to spend more time thinking about and talking to others about partners, in an effort to make sense of things or to try to 'fix' them, than to address issues directly by thinking and talking together. But relationships are more successful when we prioritise thinking and talking together.

Finally, there is *Agreeing*, which is, in a nutshell, the extent to which a couple feel they are in consensus with one another—and whether they are both happy with this.

Agreeing is about harmony, unity, and concurrence. And this applies to all aspects of their lives—how much sex they have, how much each of them works or doesn't work, how many children they have, holidays, health, wider family issues, and so on. Agreeing is about bringing together two lives and both people being happy with the amount of consensus they have.

None of us agree, or have consensus, all the time; it will vary from one day to another and one relationship to another. One couple will be in agreement most of the time, while another may not agree on a number of things, large and small. But this may not matter, if the other three togethering components are working for them.

Agreement within a relationship, like the other components, can be disturbed by outside events. Something happens, say the birth of a child, and the couple that was happy about the fact that they didn't agree most of the time, now feel unhappy about it.

Sometimes, what goes wrong is their agreement on one specific issue, so that they no longer agree over something that is important to them, because something has shifted and so their overall consensus is thrown out of balance.

These four components of togethering are a barometer of what is going on in a relationship, a way into discovering the origin of their feelings around appreciation, support, and understanding.

Of all four components, the most important is Engaging. When relationships are in trouble, the first aspect to consider is the quality of a couple's engagement. It may be the source of trouble, either because partners feel dissatisfied with the way in which they engage with each other, or because they don't realise that the way in which they engage is preventing them from feeling satisfied. Underlying satisfaction is the result of the sense of security and trust that partners have from their experience of engaging with one another. When their engagement is effective they can generally maintain a balance, irrespective of the challenges they face in navigating pressures that come up in the other areas of togethering.

Most of our lived experience involves us making constant decisions for ourselves and each decision calls upon, to a greater or lesser degree, a complex combination and process of thoughts, feelings, and bodily sensations, with meanings constructed from our experience in the present moment and the past. We might all eat, but the process by which we decide on what we eat, when and how much, and even at what speed, is uniquely personal.

Our partnerships need to be able to hold the partners' processes so that they are accommodated to their satisfaction. If one of the partners is not satisfied it is an unsatisfactory relationship.

Firstly, let's look at an unsatisfactory example:

It's a bodily sensation that comes first, a grumble from the stomach, an image comes of a really tasty poached egg at breakfast time, it leads to a smile thinking about how your partner had egg dripping down their chin and like an automaton you glance at your watch and see it is 11.45, and then comes the thought that it is soon time for lunch. With the word lunch comes a memory of a warm, sunny day and an outdoor lunch with the family, there's the feel of the sun on your face, the joyous laughter of your sister, the concentration on your father's face as he serves pasta. 'Oh yes the pasta,' you think, 'it was a cold pasta with fresh tomatoes, mozzarella and basil along with some home-made olive oil. Yes, that wonderful family holiday in Italy.' Happiness turns to sadness as the image of the memorial tree you planted for your father comes to mind. At that moment your partner comes into the room, you sense from their speed of movement and question that they are feeling under pressure and they say, 'What shall we have for lunch?'

There is a sensation of being pulled away from the tree, a kind of surrender as you leave the tree and come back into the present, feeling a little shaken and struggling to find composure. You manage to say, 'pasta with tomatoes, mozzarella and basil,' and as you speak you hear yourself and think that you have spoken with more force than you would normally. You spot a flash of annoyance across your partner's face: 'we don't have tomatoes,' followed by, 'it's not the right time of year for good tomatoes, why do you have to make everything so complicated?' You feel a stab of hurt and sadness; you long to be back in that garden. Now feeling overwhelmed and unable to think clearly you remain stuck as your partner tuts and leaves the room. Alone, the memory of that tree resurfaces, followed by sadness as your father's smiling face comes back to mind, and as it fades a feeling of intense loneliness descends on you.

As this example shows, there is so much going on underneath the few words that were exchanged, so much was missed, and a misunderstanding that was painful for both partners occurred. So, what do I mean by saying our partnerships need to be able to hold these processes? I see this as thinking about the need for the process to be shared, so let's re-run the example where this happens.

It's a bodily sensation that comes first, a grumble from the stomach, an image comes of a really tasty poached egg at breakfast time, it leads to a smile thinking about how your partner had egg dripping down their chin and like an automaton you glance at your watch and see it is 11.45, and then comes the thought that it is soon time for lunch. With the word lunch comes a memory of a warm, sunny day and an outdoor lunch with the family, there's the feel of the sun on your face, the joyous laughter of your sister, the concentration on your father's face as he serves pasta. 'Oh yes the pasta,' you think, 'it was a cold pasta with fresh tomatoes, mozzarella and basil along with some home-made olive oil. Yes, that wonderful family holiday in Italy.' Happiness turns to sadness as the image of the memorial tree you had planted for you father comes to mind.

At that moment your partner comes into the room, you sense from their speed of movement and question that they are feeling under pressure and they say, 'Hungry?'

There is a sensation of being pulled away from the tree, a kind of surrender as you leave the tree and come back into the present; feeling a little shaken and struggling to find composure and you only manage to say, 'Ummm'. Your partner says, 'Are you okay?' And with just those few seconds you're feeling less shaken and more composed. 'I was hungry and then I remembered a family lunch years ago, I was thinking of my father and ended up feeling sad, right when you came in.' Your partner says, 'Sad? You must miss him.' Your eyes feel wet and you nod but then your stomach grumbles and the word hungry comes back to your mind. 'Yes, I am hungry. You too?' Your partner says, 'Absolutely but I'm feeling under pressure as I have a meeting in half an hour, so I was thinking about a quick sandwich. Do you have something in mind?'

'I was just remembering the pasta with fresh tomatoes we ate at that lunch with my father.' Your partner looks amused. 'Hmmm tomatoes, if only it was August and we were in Italy.' You laugh, 'Yes let's get a sandwich.' In the five minutes spare between eating and your partner's meeting they look at you and say, 'I'm thinking about your dad and Italy and tomatoes.' At that moment it feels as if there are only the two of you, it is the complete opposite of loneliness—communion, if you will, and as that moment passes you feel a sense of ease and tranquility.

Sharing process means simply that you both start with the emphasis on how you are and *not* what to do. Starting with how you are enables you to work together to assess what will work for you both and the most successful relationships are those where partners help each other with their process. For example, on deciding on a time to be somewhere, one partner might know that when stressed their partner always underestimates how long it will take to get to places. So, in sharing the process, the partner with the stress/time blind spot can be reminded of it.

As I've said previously, I always encourage partners to have an explicit understanding around wanting feedback, and to invite each other to give it, and being prepared to do so even when there is a chance that at times of stress it might not be easily received.

So often couples in trouble talk about the need for compromise, but what they mean by that is that one of them should accept what the other one wants to do, while also arguing about each other's blind spots, not thinking that maybe a solution would be to agree to help each other. For me, compromise comes from sharing process to find a solution.

Sharing process is often enough to ensure relationships are better together. Sometimes, however, partners miss something of importance about the relationship that they are constructing together. That's why relationships can be considered through a framework that enables us to think about their uniqueness in relation to common properties: Being, Doing, Engaging and Agreeing.

Chapter Three

Relationships in Trouble

A felt sense of shock, hurt, and frustration; questions come to mind—*How can they do that? How can they say that?* Then sadness, anger, and maybe even hopelessness follow: hopelessness, because what has surfaced feels impossible. Perhaps it is not a new experience, but a familiar one. Such situations arise time and time again, and try as you might—talking about them, not talking about them, trying to avoid them—here you are again.

In thinking about the relationship, your feelings are best summed up as those of alienation; perhaps the words unsupported, unappreciated, misunderstood come to mind. You remember those moments when there has been a felt sense of communion, a kind of spiritual connection between you both, and you wonder whether you were mistaken, and whether it is you or your partner who has changed, or whether something has been lost.

Difficulties can emerge at any time in a relationship. You may have been together for a few weeks, months, years, or even decades when you begin to be aware that something has gone wrong. What troubles you may be no more than a feeling of unease, based on a sense that perhaps you and your partner have drifted apart, have less to say to each other, or don't do things together the way you once did. It may be due to a deterioration in the felt sense of ease between you, with increasing conflicts and unpleasant interactions. Perhaps the cause of difficulties arises from a flashpoint—an event such as the discovery of infidelity or debt— telling you that what you thought was a barely visible fault line in the values and beliefs you share is actually a gaping chasm. Possibly you have had the thought that you no longer want your relationship: it is as if a switch has been thrown and you are seeing your relationship and your partner completely differently, while they cannot understand what has happened.

Commonly, partners arrive in the therapy room citing concerns such as communication, sexual problems, infidelity, feeling unappreciated, misunderstood or unsupported, annoying behaviours, anger and, increasingly often, inequality, as the issues that have led to relationship fracture.

There is a sense of disappointment and frustration and there may be anxiety too about what has gone wrong. *Which of us is at fault? Why can't we resolve it?* As you focus on the problems, it can seem as if the person that you fell for and wanted to be with, who seemed so ideal in the first days of being together, has become someone else altogether—someone you can't communicate with, who doesn't understand you, and who at times doesn't appear to care about how you feel. And all those thoughts hurt.

When there is something wrong in a relationship, there is always pain involved, and while pain can bring both partners closer together when they are able to understand each other's distress, not understanding only serves to create distance and disconnection. When we are trying desperately to find a way out, it is both immensely difficult and often counter-intuitive to seek the answer together.

What both people in a relationship that is suffering ultimately want is to get back the felt sense of communion that they had at the start, but the pain they are experiencing means that their faith and sense of trust in that possibility are challenged. Maybe they have tried to speak to each other without success, or they find that they are just unable to broach the problem. The resulting fear means that they are likely to feel they can't talk to one another about what is wrong, and so they fall back on themselves, each trying to figure out alone what is going on. In doing so, the other partner and the relationship are both excluded.

Both partners may work hard individually to make sense of the situation, but the problem with trying to sort it out in your head is that you can only get so far before you get stuck with an anxiety that the relationship is somehow not okay, or not normal. And this anxiety, if not expressed and resolved, can grow. So, the partners get stuck and, until something happens to break the status quo, the pain and sense of disconnection escalates.

In therapy, I help couples to see and understand that they are both in pain, and in doing so they feel empathy for one another: a feeling they had started to believe was no longer possible. It is that realisation that enables couples to find their way back together again. When one sees and feels the other one's pain, they want that to stop. Recognising that they both share the desire for the other's pain to end creates an opening that can allow them to find a way forward. They may once again feel loved, but often, more importantly, comes the realisation that they are able to love again.

So, how are the seeds of trouble sewn?

At the start of a relationship, in those heady early days when two people first meet, feel drawn to one another and are in the process of deciding that they want to be together, there is a strong desire to learn all about one another, to understand one another, and to share appreciation and support. We ask all kinds of questions, we try to memorise one another's favourite ice-cream flavour or colour or taste in music, and we take note of one another's preferences, ideas, and dreams. We know from what we have learned from being with others in our lives that understanding, appreciation, and support are what make all relationships work, and so we try hard to offer those things.

There is so much at stake for us at that early stage. We want to know if we are compatible and the importance of what a relationship means in our lives will be reflected in the time and energy we put into those early stages. We tend to have a mental shopping list and to tick off the signals that tell us this person might be right for us. If we laugh at the same jokes, for example, or like the same kinds of films, share political beliefs, or both enjoy going out. We might also notice the ways in which the other person is different from us, perhaps by seeing their strength, confidence or ability to listen as desirable traits that we aspire to ourselves, or perceiving other traits as weaknesses.

We want certainty about what the relationship might be like, so we take note of things that indicate similar hopes and dreams, for example, wanting to live in the country, wanting children, feeling that career is important or being willing to work and save towards goals. As we focus on understanding the other person, we are alert to misunderstandings, and whether these are talked about or not will put in place a pattern of behaviour that will be crucial to the co-creation of the relationship and its potential to endure.

All relationships can be located on a continuum of understanding. Everyone has their own experiences of what understanding in relationships means and therefore their expectations will vary. For example, partners will often talk in therapy about how they have noticed differences in communication styles and apparent levels of understanding in each other's families. But what tends to be most important is the level of understanding the partners believe they have with one another and their jointly felt experience of ataraxy.

The understanding that develops between two people is somewhere on a continuum between being explicitly spoken or implicit, and it forms the basis of the relationship; a kind of mutually understood agreement that you both want to be together, that there is an understanding between you that brings the feelings of communion and ease.

When there is understanding we are able to show appreciation and support, because when we understand we are able to see a person's needs and work together to take those into account. Take for example the person who is always late. You find their tardiness annoying and even hurtful, you take it personally—until the first time you go to meet their family, when you notice that no one is there at the agreed meeting time, no one expects to meet at that time, but when everyone does turn up there is a sense of joy, harmony, and love. Suddenly, your partner's tardiness makes sense: you understand where it comes from and so you have a sense of appreciation. At this point, communication is possible between you, which leads to a solution that takes both of you into account.

When things go wrong, the relationship shifts its position on the understanding continuum in a way that causes a rupture.

Most of the time, the shift is towards a sense of less understanding but, sometimes, greater understanding can also lead to conflict. For example, a couple might come to understand that they are in very different places about an issue, such as having children or their beliefs around parenting. Once a problem has set in and one or both partners feel a sense of disconnect, they lose the feeling of appreciation for each other and no longer know how to support them. They may begin to think that they're in a bad relationship, making a mess of things, or stuck, with no idea how to put things right. Not being able to pinpoint the misunderstandings means that things feel wrong on the most fundamental of levels.

So, how does this happen?

Simply put, life happens. The first stage of any relationship depends upon so many factors, from how and who the partners were when they met, how they got on, how much time and energy they had to give, what else was going on for them, and what happened to them after they met. And so they settle into a relationship with various assumptions, based on what they learned at the beginning.

Over time, change reveals new aspects of others and ourselves, and challenges our capacity for understanding. Our sense of ease with what we understand and the ability for us to commune are in constant flux. When we first meet, a moment of communion might be when your hands accidentally touch as you both reach for a door handle; decades later it might be catching each other's eye as a grandchild makes you both laugh. So, change can bring you both closer, but it can also reveal or reinforce misunderstandings.

Sometimes, things become intolerable following an event or during a time of stress and upheaval. Problems at work, new opportunities, redundancy, ill health, moving home, building extensions, financial difficulties, losses, fertility and IVF (In Vitro Fertilisation), the arrival of a new child, year-long pandemic and lockdown restrictions, ageing parents and family issues can all bring pressures that can either exacerbate misunderstandings or be the source of them.

Misunderstandings can come from the partners not being able to understand each other's communications; this is not necessarily what is said or how, but more about how the partners experience each other. For example, tiredness might be mistaken for irritation, quietness for happiness, a smile as a sign of joy rather than nervousness and, crucially, the difficulty in understanding underlying feelings when anger is expressed.

In those early days of a relationship, when it's all too easy to internalise 'rules', misunderstandings can arise that may cause problems later. If one partner says they don't like something, or don't want to do it then the other can conclude that this is the way it's going to be, and that that activity is no longer an option. This can become the status quo for years to come.

Imagine a new couple talking about the kind of holidays they like. Ari says, 'I can't stand beach holidays.' Zene thinks that means beach holidays are out, and it isn't really discussed again. Over the years, Zene begins to feel resentful: he loved beach holidays before they met and finds that images of the beach come to mind during the day and in dreams. Zene feels that there's been no compromise attempted. In their communications, Zene may be saying something like, 'You are so inflexible,' while Ari may be saying, 'You don't let me say what I want.' They don't even recognise the origin of the problem and so it becomes inevitable that not only does the problem remain, but also every time they have the same interaction, the hurt feelings mount. And they will have that interaction again and again and again.

In this way, a casual statement about what is true at a certain point in time can crystallise into a rule. The problem with that is that one partner may begin to think, *Why is it me giving in? I really miss beach holidays.* Perhaps, eventually, the relationship comes under strain. Zene, feeling exasperated, might complain, 'You never wanted to go on a beach holiday'. Ari replies, 'Oh, did I say that? I don't even remember saying it. Beach holidays aren't my thing, but I don't mind going on one if it's what you would like. What about a city where there is a beach, like Rio?'

When they talk about it, Ari and Zene realise that not going on a beach holiday didn't matter to Ari nearly as much as Zene imagined it did. In this way, a long-standing source of frustration for the relationship was resolved.

Such a scenario can occur many times in many ways. Often, something one partner imagines or assumes about the relationship sets in early on and is not adapted or changed because it hasn't been expressed, or because the situation is thought of as in the past and they have decided to try to put it behind them.

It's only when a couple is able to track the source of the misunderstanding that partners can begin to understand what is going on for one another. Paying attention to one another and realising that one of them is hurting, rather than just angry or distant, leads to different choices and genuine compromises. Often the presenting issue doesn't matter as much as the resentment and distance that has entered the relationship and the resulting feelings that arise as thoughts about the relationship failing.

To complicate matters there's a very common fantasy that we should know what our partner is thinking, often reinforced by an explicit or implicit message that says, 'If I've got to tell you what I'm thinking then perhaps you don't care about me.' That, of course, goes both ways.

As children many of us learn to know what our parents and other adults are thinking. They actually expect this of us, as in 'You know it's bedtime', 'You know it's time to get dressed', 'You know not to run in the corridors', and so on. Once a child has been told what to do a number of times, parents and other adults will then expect the child to have learned what they are supposed to do without having to be told again. And children do learn, because they pay great attention to parents and other adults. Their vulnerability means that those relationships, ones that they do not get to choose, really matter. These are relationships with a power dynamic created by norms and societal structures about parental responsibility, whereas our adult friendships and romantic relationships can, if we choose, be free of power.

Interestingly, it was only in 1980 that the Anglican Church gave a couple the option not to use 'obey' in the standard bride's vows and only in 2000 did 'obey' become something a couple would have to ask to include. Anyone married before

2000 therefore exists in a marriage whereby a power imbalance was explicit.

A relationship between adults, unlike the one between a child and an adult, is a relationship between equals who have joint responsibility. It is the internalised beliefs and values around relationships that will determine the nature of the relationship.

You might think that you should know what your partner is thinking, or that they should know what you are thinking—but *why*? Such an idea is a myth, a fantasy that keeps us trapped in an unhelpful position. Both partners need to release themselves from that trap by accepting that they can have a deep understanding with another person and still not know what they are thinking: it's your joint responsibility to ensure understanding. In partial terms, that means each partner should always think about the understanding that exists; trying to be aware of what they need to share but also knowing when to seek clarification.

One of the most common experiences in therapy is that someone expects their partner to know what they want, and yet when they are asked what it is that they want, they realise they don't know. It brings me back to the expectation that seems to have gained currency in today's culture: that we can know others better than they know themselves.

The pain of disconnection can become much worse if there are difficult and nasty arguments, misunderstandings piled on top of one another, defensiveness, and aggression. If both partners feel hurt and misunderstood, it is difficult to get to the underlying concerns. Feeling that you're making a mess of things, that you've got something wrong, is painful. There is pain from the initial problem and then further pain that comes from being unable to find a resolution.

When this happens, what do we do?

Most people, initially, try to communicate that there is a problem. They may know exactly what it is, or it may be that they just have a sense of unease, a feeling that something has changed, or is missing. They may use silence, brooding, a shrug, or a huff to indicate that they feel should be understood by the other. Or they may try to talk about the problem. Putting such thoughts into words can be difficult however, and often they find that the process of talking about their experience in the relationship is either too painful or not helpful. It can be difficult to find words that bring understanding for both partners and so defensiveness can come into play, with one partner feeling accused and the other accusing.

Timing is almost always crucial. Finding a time when the partners are feeling relaxed and have energy for engagement will often be the only factor that lies between finding resolution or further conflict. Often, trouble is exacerbated because one partner believes in immediate communication while the other prefers to arrange to speak later. Again, understanding each other in this regard can enable a couple to find a way that works for both.

Silenced by a put-down, an argument, or feeling unheard, one partner can be left with something on their mind that is troubling them. Unable to process it and unsure what to do with it, they suppress feelings that can build up to the point where what might have been very resolvable begins to feel like a make-or-break issue.

Sometimes, both partners will lapse into a hopeless silence. Convinced that there is no point in trying to talk or change things in the relationship, they settle for apathy, for getting on with the things they have to do—work, parenting, paying the bills—while suppressing the longing to find a reconnection with one another. It can become the status quo for months and even years.

When talking doesn't work, communication can shut down, with one or both partners feeling misunderstood. At this stage, it is often the case that they will seek to find a problem in the way they communicate, finding fault with one another. One might say the other doesn't talk enough, while the other might say that the first one talks too much, and that they can't keep up. Both might insist that the other is a poor communicator who should improve, and when that doesn't work, desperation often leads to each thinking about the partner in pathological terms: are they suffering from ASD (Autistic Spectrum Disorder), ADHD (Attention Deficit Hyperactivity Disorder), narcissism, or are they bipolar?

The question I ask when I see two people in pain is, 'What can the relationship do differently here to support both partners?'

When Hao told Eilian that, having reached a certain stage in their lives, they should have a second home in the country, Eilian responded with, 'Oh, you're all about second homes in the country aren't you?' Feeling put down, Hao said nothing more. What was lost in the moment was that the 'second home in the country' was really a metaphor for how life should feel at that stage. Not so much that there should actually be a second home, but rather that there was something missing. If Eilian had responded in a way that opened up discussion, they might have been able to talk about it. At the same time, what Hao missed was that Eilian also felt there was something not quite right with the relationship: Eilian's snappy response was a way of approaching the subject. Often, a couple both feel the same concern, but it is hidden behind their different approaches.

It is natural to locate pain and blame in those with whom we struggle for the simple fact that they are there in front of us. We often lash out with a put-down or a criticism of those to whom we are closest. Hurt demands that we act fast, looking for the source of the pain and, as neuroscience has shown, it is some seconds before our cognitive functions catch up and we are able to think, or try to understand. In this way, Eilian responded instantly to the words 'second home' rather than thinking about what it might mean for Hao. In response and feeling hurt, Hao shut down, not thinking that Eilian might be making a point too.

This pain response means that it is not in the least surprising that the tendency is often to blame and to use unhelpful labels and terms that, if expressed out loud, often only result in the other person feeling judged, misunderstood, and unfairly blamed.

Defensiveness can be a major obstacle to open communication. Many of us try not to be defensive when we feel upset because we think we are being criticised, and criticism often demands change. When it comes to change, we are naturally cautious: we need to know that the change will be positive, and we need to know what we need to do and that we have the energy to do it. If we're going to have to start doing something that we can't really imagine ourselves doing, then change will not be possible and we will defend against it. And when we are defensive the situation tends to escalate. The other person often becomes defensive too and situations can very quickly become so emotionally intense that any helpful communication becomes impossible.

Our defensiveness is about fear; we are afraid of being judged and, more importantly, of making changes that ultimately are not sustainable.

We live in a world where there's a huge amount of pressure to fulfil all our potential and become everything we are capable of being. We want to be the best partner, employee, boss, family member, or parent that we can be. So, feeling that we have somehow got things wrong is painful, especially in our closest relationship, and if we start to feel criticised or misunderstood then that hurts too.

All too often an argument about an unresolved issue may result in one partner saying to the other, 'Well, you just don't care,' and this always hurts. None of us want to be seen as someone who doesn't care: that's not the way we think of ourselves. But so often the accusation of not caring is the result of a misunderstanding that leads to a breakdown in appreciation and the impossibility of being supportive.

The way we care and love other people is central to us, so what causes us pain is that we're not able to find a way of living that realises our potential. If we get a bad assessment at work the hurt comes not solely from thinking that we have a mean boss (though we might do), but also from the idea that we're not performing as well as we could be or that we have chosen the wrong career. And it's the same in our relationships.

We have many ways of showing that we care, and within a relationship those ways can be very different. For one person it might be cleaning up the home. For another, the clean house might be unimportant—their idea of caring might be cuddling up together in front of a good film. This can very easily be a source of misunderstanding, with one person believing that they have shown they care and the other, oblivious to it, expecting something very different.

In one of my first training sessions in relationship therapy, our group of twenty or so therapists were asked to write down a word that we associated with the way love was demonstrated in our families growing up. It was a revelation for me because there were almost twenty different answers. Love is a word that often comes up in therapy, so when two people are saying that they don't feel loved, an exploration of what love means for each of them is really important.

Sometimes, the inability to communicate in a satisfactory way results in an escalation by one partner or the other, which forces the issue out into the open. This is often the scenario behind infidelity. Initially, powerful feelings are unlikely to be conducive to communication, but when the partner who feels betrayed is able to ask what went wrong, the other might say, 'Well, we weren't having enough sex.' Again, strong feelings are likely to surface initially, but given time the first partner might then be able to respond, 'I know we didn't have a lot of sex, but I thought you were okay with that.' If they are able to explore what has gone wrong, they may realise that the issue wasn't sex at all: it was fun, closeness, playfulness—the things that were present in the relationship at the beginning, but which got lost because the routines and chores took over.

For some couples agreeing not to agree is fine and they accept the situation as it is: 'You want more sex, I want less sex, we've gone round in circles and it's something we can't do anything about. Fine, we've got so much else going for us, we can live with this.'

However, if unresolved disappointment remains, for one or both of them, then they haven't got to the point of accepting their differences and finding a genuine compromise. The issue then becomes a concern that the couple isn't able to work through together, and one of them is left holding something and feeling uncertain about what to do about it. It's this uncertainty that causes pain. And if one partner in a relationship is in pain then both partners are in a painful relationship.

One of the things people worry about when thinking about their relationship issues is that they're going to have to change in some way and, as previously mentioned, we don't like to change because we know how complicated it can be for us: one small change can cause big problems. It can feel like a domino effect: you change where you put your wallet at home and suddenly you find you're at work without your wallet and it throws the whole day out. So, there may well be a fear that change is not possible for either partner. Whereas in actual fact the change might be to realise that they don't need to change; their fear about the relationship is just a fear.

Nour's partner, Quin, said, 'You need to learn to talk about your feelings.' Up until that point, not talking about feelings hadn't been a problem: now, Nour's partner wants change and says it is Nour's responsibility. Nour says, 'It's only you who doesn't understand, I think you should learn about how not to do things that hurt other people's feelings.'

Or take Valo, who has always been a bit of a perfectionist and thought it was perfectly all right to be so. While stressful at times, the approach had helped him achieve good exam results and enjoy a successful career. Valo's partner Blair admired those perfectionist traits at the start of their relationship, but a few years later began to criticise Valo for being obsessive about getting everything right. *Well, yes*, Valo might think, *that's how I've always been, why is it now a problem? Ho*w can I change the way I am? Do I want to change the way I am?

In this way the partners take positions, each believing that theirs has merit. However, what is being missed is that the problem exists not in each other, although they can both probably improve and develop their relationship skills, but in the relationship they have created and how misunderstandings can be located within it.

In setting out to resolve issues in the relationship the first thing to know is that any kind of struggle within a relationship is there because the relationship is there. Two separate individuals have come together to form a relationship and it is because this relationship exists that there is the potential for misunderstanding and disagreement, and hurt, as well as for love, sharing, and fulfilment. When issues arise, it is because the relationship is not able to accommodate both people's needs and not because either of the two people in the relationship is wrong or lacking in some way. Something is not working.

To re-establish the feeling of connection with one another two things need to be dealt with: the wounds created by the misunderstandings and the misunderstandings themselves. Willingness on both sides and a sense of potential progress can rebuild trust in the relationship and help couples move towards a felt sense of understanding, appreciation, and support. When this is present, the words *love* and *communing* both feel appropriate and the word *ataraxy* sums up how they feel when reflecting on the relationship.

So, when I meet partners for the first time and hear about what brings them to me, I can often sense the fear and desperation. Therapy might appear to be a last resort and partners can feel almost jolted into it because of the magnitude of a triggering event, such as an infidelity. Getting past the event will need both of them to be able to put the event itself to one side so that the underlying misunderstandings can be uncovered.

Once this has happened, the extent to which understanding is then achieved often determines whether they will be able to move beyond the event itself.

Chapter Four

Getting Better Together

It's a feeling of release like surrender but not defeat; like achievement but not conquering. It's like having reached the limit of something and for that limit to suddenly have no significance, or that moment of recognition when you awaken from a dream. It's followed by sudden lightness—a moment of warmth and of optimism. It is an experience of a shift in energy; a chink of light that allows a brief sense that something, perhaps almost imperceptibly, has changed.

This chink, where light can enter, is what is needed when the relationship feels stuck. When this happens, it is the starting point for moving forward; you are again in charge and can choose a different path. From a new feeling comes a new thought, or image, and from this comes possibility. From possibility comes hope, and from hope comes energy. Without energy nothing can change, while with energy so much is possible. But the moment doubt reappears you can slip back, and that momentary relief, the curiosity, that unexplainable blip or anomaly, and the truth it contains, can be lost.

Such moments reveal the point at which we experience something as tolerable or intolerable; something that either detracts or contributes to our wellbeing. Before our illnesses were differentiated into physical and psychological, the Greek word 'dis-ease' (disease) expressed the felt experience of not being at ease. Today, I see the field of therapy as being concerned with the 'dis-ease' that remains once modern medicine has deployed its full armoury.

Unlike medicine that intervenes in a physical way, relying on something external to the sufferer, therapy facilitates the sufferer in the deployment of their own intervention, so the process whereby 'dis-ease' moves into experiencing 'ease' can be seen as coming from a moment of relief, insight, revelation, or acceptance and as the passing into a felt sense of calm, tranquility, and equanimity. It's about seeing things for what they are and, as a result, being able to find a way forward. For me, the words that most make sense of the experience from dis-ease to ease are *epoche* and *ataraxy*—both of which I have mentioned previously. In therapy, by attending effectively to dis-ease we come to a moment of *epoche*, one that opens the way to *ataraxy*.

Repetitive patterns that have been established between you—conversations, perhaps attempted negotiations or silences—will resume and nothing will be different unless you give that moment of *epoche* the attention it deserves. By that I mean that when you spot one of those moments, don't let it slip by unheeded: notice it, hold onto it, give it your attention, and think about it. What was going on that enabled something different to happen? Think of such a moment as significant; that it makes a difference and provides an opening for change. Save and savour such moments.

As a therapist, I often find that I act as a caretaker of those moments, and I wonder about them at times when the partners return to their usual interactions. Such moments are, I am certain, a tool for change, if change is what the partners want. In therapy, I will often remind partners of those moments, enquire as to how they are making sense of them and encourage them to become curious about them, because this is the way of moving from impossibility towards possibility.

You may have discussed an issue, a perceived problem, many times. But if a conversation has been had more than once then it hasn't been had at all. By this I mean that if you keep talking about something in the same way and nothing changes, then talking, or the way in which you are talking, is not resolving it. Let's take the example of lateness. If one person is always late and the other is annoyed by it and they have talked about it many times without the pattern of lateness and annoyance changing, then a different conversation needs to happen.

The recognition that something different needs to happen is the first step towards resolution. Not everyone wants or is ready for such a move. Pain in a relationship can be a bit like toothache; for some people a twinge of toothache is enough to send them hurrying to the dentist. Conversely, others may tolerate a low level of nagging pain for quite some time before they are ready to put themselves in the dentist's chair. Additionally, our positions in relation to others also help us to make sense of who we are in the world and enable us to make decisions. For example, 'family should always come first' will mean that family gets prioritised. When a family member has a different position, however—for example, 'my friends are my chosen family'—the conflict that arises is not about right and wrong but about protecting our sense of identity and the meaning we have constructed that enables us to feel at greatest ease.

Often, the decision to seek something different that will shift things in the relationship comes down to a trade-off between the situation as it is and what it might be if we seek to change it, because we know that change is something that always has consequences. We can hope things are going to be better, but we can't be certain. So sometimes the thought will be: *Do I carry on with the relationship as it is? It's not so bad, better than my parents', better than my friends' and, after all, no one has a perfect relationship. Or do I try to tackle this, and if I do will it make things better or might it make them worse?* And, paradoxically, isn't a decision *not* to do something also a way of tackling the situation?

Paradox can confront us with the absurdity of our positions. For example, the family member who claims to put family first is required to accept the family member who does not hold that position, otherwise they are not living congruently. We know that we are full of contradictions, but in relationships conflict only arises when empathy for the existence of those contradictions is eroded.

So, initially there is a decision to be made about whether to continue to tolerate things. If one person is unhappy in a relationship, then it's an unhappy relationship, so conversation between partners at this stage can be valuable. If you are willing to say, 'I know that I'm not happy about this aspect of our relationship and yet I'm uncertain about whether it will help us if we change it,' then you may get a response that agrees, or one that sees things as much worse, or far better, than your view. And your partner's response may influence your decision. If they feel things are much better in the relationship than you do, you may find that reassuring. That might mean there is less pressure to bring about change, because if you've talked about it and your partner is happy, then it might feel more tolerable for you. On the other hand, if your partner feels change is definitely needed then this may allow you to decide together to do something different.

If you decide that something in the relationship is not working and that you want to create the conditions for change, then something new is needed. If at that point there is a sense of hopelessness, resignation or impossibility, how is it possible to open a crack and allow in the light that might lead you to something new?

I think of it as the need to apply optimal pressure to the situation. With optimal pressure, we apply ourselves adequately enough to allow change without the need to break. As an example, take threading a needle. Perhaps you try several times, but it's impossible to get the thread through the eye of the needle. What next? You ease off and try something different— putting the light on, changing sitting position, using your glasses, licking the thread to make it smoother—and then, just when you thought it was impossible, the thread goes straight through the eye of the needle with an ease that leads you to wonder whether it was entirely of your own doing. In this way, optimal pressure is just enough to bring about the change you want.

When partners come to therapy they are together in a different space, a third person in the room, and some conditions are agreed. In this way, therapy can provide the difference that allows for change. So, going to a therapist is one way of recognising that something different is required. It involves taking charge of the process of creating the conditions in which change can happen.

Before it is possible to find the chink of light, you need to know where the difficulties lie. In my experience, partners often come to therapy believing that they know what the problem is. And while that can be the starting point, it always leads to something else.

As a therapist I look to understand the relationship by applying a framework that creates optimal pressure, illuminating areas for attention and identifying the source of ruptures, the ways that these can be healed, and the skills that need to be introduced or developed.

The starting point is always to understand the partners' differing perspectives about the concerns they have and also what they would like to happen. And then I will want to ensure we build a joint understanding as to how it is that whatever matters to each person has come to matter. To take the earlier example of type of holiday: a beach holiday isn't necessarily about one person's preference taking priority over another—it can also be about what is needed in order for the person to feel properly rested and to keep well. As we explore the meanings behind the partners' concerns, I will be thinking about the partners' individual ways of living and their styles of striving and the resulting relationship that is created. Our individual ways of living can be considered alongside broader aspects of daily life that we all experience.

At the same time, I attend to the uniqueness of the relationship that is created by the partners' decision to be together, and I consider the relationship through the framework that I call *togethering*. I use this word as it describes clearly that what is being considered is the 'ing' that is lived through being together. It is the unique existence and living of the relationship and its striving. As with our individual experience of living, the broad aspects of togethering are also considered. The four main aspects I think about, as outlined in chapter two, are: Being (the amount of time spent together); Doing (the amount of energy in the relationship); Engaging (the ways in which the partners interact); and Agreeing (the degree to which the partners agree on the way to live in terms of the five main pillars of relationships, spirituality, health, security, and interests).

Finally, I think about how I am in relation to the partners, both individually and in the togethering created by the therapeutic relationship. Specifically, I look at how my experiences of communion and alienation differ with each partner, and the source of that in relation to the main pillars. In thinking about my experience of being with the partners together, I examine how I experience time, energy, our interactions, and the sense of agreement or disagreement. Furthermore, I am called upon to take into account my own way of living and striving so that I am always asking myself if my thoughts and feelings are serving the therapy.

The aspects of Being (time) and Doing (energy) are in some ways the most straightforward to identify, as they are aspects of living that we can all broadly relate to. However, specific aspects that I look out for with regard to time include how both partners feel about the amount of time spent together and whether there is a focus of time that appears relevant. Some relationships struggle because of things that have happened in the past, while others face difficulties because partners struggle with how they are together in the present moment. Meanwhile, some couples struggle because of differing views about the future. In assessing the state of a relationship, it can be helpful to think about not just the present moment but also the past and the future.

Meanwhile, energy tends to come into play at times when a change for one of the partners means an impact on the relationship. Times of transition can be significant; physical illness is an obvious one, but depression is also something that can have a devastating impact on togethering.

Engaging and Agreeing are naturally more complex, given the diversity of how we place differing emphasis on life's main pillars, and therefore on how we live and our styles of striving. As mentioned previously, those differences come from the unique societal and relationship systems created by cultures, religions, geographies, families, and our own individual systems.

One of the ways in which I think about concerns in all areas is through reflection on the role I feel drawn to in our togethering. Am I finding myself acting as a witness, a referee, a facilitator, or a mediator? A witness can be affirming for both partners when a conversation needs to take place. A referee can say, 'Time out, this is not helping.' A facilitator will say, 'Hold on, you're not understanding each other because you're not hearing each other.' And a mediator will say, 'What are you both able to settle on here, to help you reach an agreement?'

In thinking here about engaging, I think about the felt sense the partners have around how they experience each other, what they understand from each other, the degree to which they speak explicitly about the relationship with each other, and also how they help each other. For example, what type of agreement partners might make when at a social event? Does one rescue his partner from a tedious conversation, while the other steers her partner gently away from the calorie-laden desert buffet?

Engaging, as with all the other aspects of togethering can, of course, be weaponised. For example, if someone knows their partner loves to talk about their day, they might refuse to engage because they are upset with another aspect of their togethering.

When I work with partners, I will consider all of these questions. I will think also about the people in the relationship as individuals, about their way of being and about how they interact in their relationship with each other as well as within the relationship as a whole, and in their individual relationships with themselves.

A simple example: Soli was always concerned with finding bargains, searching out the cheapest brands or the best multiple offers. Partner Pavo would do this too when they were together, but found it stressful. Later, Pavo said that when shopping alone, it was a relief not to be searching out the bargains. In identifying this one, seemingly small, difference between them served to enable conversations around their different ways of constructing meaning. For Soli, who grew up in a family where finances were stretched, time spent looking for bargains brought a sense of security because in the past it had ensured that everyone in the family had enough to eat. For Pavo, who grew up in an environment where there was money but a pressure on time together, and whose father could be very aggressive if the family missed mealtimes together, limiting time at the supermarket brought a sense of security.

Both Soli and Pavo shared their desire for security in their family, but they misunderstood each other's actions. Soli and Pavo's behaviours, when considered through the lens of attitudes towards money, only served to focus on their differences, but identifying what money meant to them revealed their shared care and concern around security and enabled them to feel safe with each other. As a result, whenever they got into conflict over shopping they were able to talk about their shopping in terms of whether they were buying enough to feed everyone and also about how much time they were taking. In this way, they were able to work together, appreciating each other's approach to shopping, understanding each other's behaviour, and supporting each other's needs.

Sometimes, the problem can be discerned through something specific. For instance, the partners might talk about how much time they are spending together. Sometimes it might be that I get a sense that there is an issue about time spent together based on what I know about the individuals as well as the couple. I will consider the five main pillars and I will also look at aspects of togethering, time spent together and apart and how they feel about it, their energy, the style and shape, both verbal and non-verbal, of their engagement and interaction, and the consensus they have around the shared aspects of their lives.

It's the combination of all that information that helps me to understand where the difficulty, or difficulties, might lie. And if I have understood their relationship—what is going on for the partners as well as for me and, crucially, what I am for them in terms of what I represent and what my potential is—then I stand a chance of making an intervention that will bring something new.

I am always aware that often we don't understand why we do things, why our partners do things, or why things happen in the relationship: we're all on a continuum of self-awareness. But at the same time, there's a striving in each of us to do the best we can, and to show that we care. If we can understand the ways in which each of us strives, and appreciate that striving and support it, then that will maintain and build the relationship.

When we are open to the possibility that there isn't a right and a wrong, when we're curious about how it is our partners do things the way they do them, and when we're open to connecting empathically, then we will discover what has gone wrong in the relationship and that this can be traced back to something we needed to understand.

When we are not open to these possibilities, this in itself can flag up other issues: Are we okay in ourselves? Is the other person okay? Is it an abusive relationship? Or is this not a relationship that we want?

As I pulled together the beliefs, ideas, and concepts that I have put forward in these chapters it occurred to me that the best way of bringing these concepts to life and illustrating the ways in which they can apply would be to present examples of partners in different situations and at different stages of their lives and relationships.

I'm grateful to have had opportunity to listen to the relationship concerns of thousands of people over the past twenty or so years. The insight and understanding that I gained from those interactions inform the stories that follow, but I want to emphasise that while the partners in these examples could be anybody, they are not *somebody*: they are not people that I have known or worked with. In putting these stories together, I was fortunate to work with a writer who was able to construct the framework of the stories, allowing me to identify the potential moments of therapeutic change and to formulate my response in each situation. We spent many hours talking about the concerns people bring to therapy and as we explored and wrote the initial chapters the ideas came about for the examples we have chosen.

All the stories follow the same construct: initial background, followed by my initial response; a sample of a therapeutic session, the moment of potential change, what happened subsequently; and finally my reflections. I have included in my response and reflections some of my personal reactions to what is happening in the therapy room, because in the field of existential psychotherapy the therapist's own experience is both relevant and informative when understanding what is happening for those who have come to therapy.

The moment of potential therapeutic change is what matters most in each case: this is when the chink of light appears, whether through my intervention, the partners' own observations, or a change in the direction of the session. In each case that is when the moment of *epoche* occurs that will lead to *ataraxy* for the two people concerned. That moment is always profound and moving and it is the catalyst for insight and choice.

The following examples are, I hope, illuminating in terms of how partners do their togethering, how misunderstandings can set in or persist, and how, with willingness and energy, real change can come about.

Story One

Bree and David

We can't get past his infidelity

The Background

Bree and David are in their forties and they have been together for ten years. Recently, David was unfaithful, and Bree found out. 'We tried to talk about it,' Bree said, 'but we got nowhere, we were both so upset. After a particularly bad row, I threw a dining room chair at the French windows and broke them, and David left the house and went to stay on a friend's couch for the night. That's when we decided we needed some help.'

'We feel completely stuck,' David said. 'We don't know whether we want to end the relationship or not. I don't think we do, but we just can't get past what happened.'

They began therapy a month ago. It was David who made the appointment with me, 'because Bree insisted'. Bree had found my details, and she thought David 'would speak more easily if we had a male therapist'. They both love dogs, having two of their own, and had seen that I worked with Holly, my chocolate Labrador, in the room, so this was also something they found encouraging.

In the first few sessions, David and Bree talked about how, in the past they had, in Bree's words, 'never really talked with each other when something was not OK between us'. However, they said, for the first seven years of their relationship they were rarely upset with each other, and life was fun and uncomplicated. They both acknowledged that there was a change about three years ago when Bree took on a new job that required her to take trips away from home and work long hours. 'I think the relationship suffered,' David said. 'We didn't find ways to adapt.'

Bree discovered David's infidelity a few weeks before they came to therapy, and it remained central to their thoughts and feelings in every interaction. Bree said, 'I can't stop thinking about David with another woman. I need to talk about things in order to feel better, but every time we try to talk we both end up feeling worse.'

When they talked about the way they met I was struck by how their different ways of being had been what connected them. Introduced at a dinner party by a mutual friend, there had been a discussion about the TV series *Mad Men*. Bree had said she would love to get a job in a leading advertising agency, while David, who had worked in advertising, said that he had left his job because of the pressure and was now much happier working as a teacher. They had a conversation about the importance of balance in life but also how hard it was to know what balance meant. In therapy, Bree admitted that she tended to 'take on too much and stay too long in difficult situations,' whereas David admitted that he could 'find it hard to stay present under too much pressure'.

In their sessions so far, I have noticed a pattern in which thoughts of the infidelity leave Bree feeling hurt, that she then thinks further about the infidelity, feels betrayed and, in her fury, demands that David say sorry. Meanwhile, David says whatever Bree wants, hoping that things will settle down as quickly as possible.

My Initial Response
In sessions I feel moments of communion with Bree when she talks about how betrayed she feels, and with David when he speaks about his bewilderment around how he ended up being a husband who had an affair.

I think also about their differing energies: Bree's gusto relative to David's calmness. I think of the possibility that, while they understand and appreciate that difference about each other when their togethering is not under stress, these differing ways of being may actually fuel misunderstanding when there is stress.

I suspect that misunderstanding confronts them with loss, and this activates Bree's fury and David's withdrawal, although I am curious to understand whether David's withdrawal comes before Bree's anger or *vice versa*.

They both seem to agree that they should be talking about the details of the infidelity. However, they are not talking about the situation leading up to it. I think they both have a sense of responsibility around the deterioration of the relationship prior to the infidelity.

They are stuck in the pain of what happened, and I'd like to see if something different can happen when the infidelity comes up. Infidelity is almost always traumatic and sometimes healing a trauma happens through revisiting the traumatic event, while at others it can heal through working to avoid revisiting the event.

Given the nature of infidelity, where one partner is often seen as or feels guilty of a wrongdoing, I also wonder about the potential for one or both of them to feel shame. Often the one who has the affair feels most shame, but partners can feel shame for being in a relationship where there was infidelity—so I wonder about Bree and David's shame and the potential impact on their being able to speak easily to each other.

In Session

We are halfway through the session. Bree has become upset and angry and has demanded an apology. David has complied.

I notice a change in Bree's behaviour: she is shifting quite a lot in her seat. David had been looking calmer, but as he is looking at Bree he too appears to be changing in his demeanour.

I start to notice in myself a feeling of discomfort and I feel myself tensing. I am expecting Bree's feeling of hurt about David's infidelity to resurface and that the hurt will become anger, directed probably at David, but perhaps also at me because, despite trusting me, she is in pain. So I am steeling myself; my senses are heightened and I am waiting for what is going to come. I also feel excited and hopeful as these are signs that a moment may arise when I might intervene in a meaningful way. I do not know how I will intervene; all I know is that I have a sense that an opportunity to disturb the unhelpful dynamic will present itself.

Bree looks up. 'My life is shit,' she says. 'I thought I had a fabulous life. And now I feel shit. And you,' she shouts at David, 'it's your fault. You've done this to me. You've destroyed me.'

She is back in her feelings of hurt, reliving the trauma. I expect David to respond in a defensive way and an escalation in their conflict.

'That's right, blame me,' David snaps back. 'That's it, all the time. And yes, okay, I have done this, but you know, I'm not going to keep saying I'm sorry.'

'You are just terrible. What would your parents think if they knew?' Bree screams.

At this point, Holly, who's been lying quietly on her bed, jumps to her feet and slinks around the back of my chair.

'You always bring my parents into it, don't you? You're just nasty,' he says.

'Yeah. Because they think they brought up a nice man, don't they? Someone who's kind and gentle. But you're nothing but a cheat.'

David slumps, looking totally defeated. He is looking at the picture of a waterfall behind me but I'm not sure he is actually seeing it. I think that while he is still there physically, psychologically he has left.

This is the moment I have been waiting for: the opportunity for me to intervene. I'm aware that it is probably very much like a replay of the moment when Bree broke the French windows and David left the house.

'Bree, David,' I say, firmly and loudly enough to gain their attention, 'I would just like to point out that what's happened here is a repeat of the pattern that your conversations take around the issue of the infidelity. You said you wanted to change this, so can I check? Is this helpful when your conversations are like this?'

Bree looks at me. 'I don't care if they're bloody helpful or not. It's helpful for me just to be able to let out my fury. I am so furious.'

'I understand you are furious, but I notice Holly has gone behind my chair so I would like to move her into another room.'

Bree looks quite shocked and then a bit sheepish. 'Oh, no, I didn't mean to . . . poor Holly, I didn't mean to upset her. I get so mad, and I just don't know what to do.'

There is a silence and then I notice that David has changed his posture, coming out of the slump and sitting more upright. He looks as though he is coming out of a trance.

'Yes,' he says. 'I know. You get so cross. And then I get so nervous, and I feel ashamed and think I am such a failure. I don't know what to do. I feel really sad to see you so upset, and it makes me want to leave.'

Bree stares intently at David. 'I didn't realise that,' she says quietly, 'I didn't know you felt that way.'

After a pause, she reaches for his hand. They make eye contact and she smiles. He smiles back and I notice her shoulders drop. I feel a change in the charge in the room—the fury and hurt has dissipated.

They both look to me.

'You share the same experience of feeling hurt and I'd like to offer the word trauma,' I say. 'Bree, your hurt turns to anger and David, while you initially try to stay present, Bree's anger results in you wanting to get away, so you both end up unsure about what to do. This is horrible for you both, but your pain is caused by the same thing—the loss of the relationship that you say was "fun and uncomplicated" until three years ago.'

They look again at each other, and I feel deeply moved: I am witnessing a private moment of intimacy—communion, if you will.

The Moment

My intervention—and Holly's—created enough of a pause to enable Bree and David to think about what was happening. Bree became aware of her impact on Holly, and then of her impact on David. David, experiencing Bree differently, was able to speak differently and that changed the understanding between them. It enabled a moment of communion and a move towards a sense of ease.

They were able to voice their individual truths and at the same time it gave me the opportunity to point out that they had both suffered a terrible loss. This relationship truth, made explicit, allowed them to experience a shared feeling and gave them an experience of their relationship as it had been—not before the infidelity, but before the career change three years previously.

What Happened Next

Bree and David returned for the next session saying that they had been much better together, kinder to one another, and more able to listen to what the other had to say.

They wanted to try to stay together but felt nervous about whether they would feel hurt again in the relationship. We used subsequent sessions to focus on getting them both used to telling each other when something was not okay and navigating their management of time and energy together, so that the relationship would be able to contain both Bree and David.

Through the therapy they were able to make sense of the infidelity as something that came from a joint failure to keep the right balance—something they had both admitted, in their first therapy session, was difficult for them. Bree's fury decreased, as did David's shame, and this enabled them to speak more easily together.

The near loss of the relationship made Bree realise that once again she had taken on too much at the cost of other areas of her life. Meanwhile, David realised that although his inclination was to withdraw and keep quiet it was actually helpful to their relationship and to Bree if he spoke up when he thought she was doing too much.

These shifts took time for both Bree and David: they were finding a new way of being together and inevitably, at times, this felt uncomfortable, but it led to greater openness and increased closeness for both of them. While the infidelity remained a wound that left a scar and had the potential to resurface at times of stress, it gradually lost its power, as Bree and David found they were able to keep the balance they needed, individually and in their relationship.

My Reflection

So often people are painfully stuck in patterns without even realising there are other possibilities. Bree's intense pain, shock, and sense of dissembling was as painful to contemplate as David's period of loneliness, his shame at his being someone who'd had an affair and his distress at the pain Bree was experiencing. Most certainly this situation brought up loss— David experienced loss as Bree's work took her away, while Bree was confronted with loss suddenly on discovery of the infidelity, after which they both faced the potential of loss of their relationship.

Bree and David's arguments about the infidelity were putting focus on their experience of alienation, when what they needed was to be talking about how the infidelity came to be, and while an infidelity cannot be undone, and their life has changed, their ability to again feel at ease together and to experience communion shows that healing is possible.

The two had initially connected around agreement on the importance of the issue of balance in their lives, and that, as an aspect of their approach to living, provided a prism through which their togethering could be viewed. When they met, their different ways of being in balance actually created a positive dynamic that worked well for them and they had a sense of ease around engagement, being able to interact without argument because of the level of satisfaction they both felt. But after Bree's change of job they both struggled, in their very different ways—a jointly held blind spot if you will—with how to maintain balance.

When the relationship lost its sense of balance, there were consequences for them both, individually and together. They were not wrong to allow a change, but they were unable to talk about it and to manage it together. If they had spoken about the ways in which Bree's new job might impact their relationship, they might have been able to agree that both would keep an eye out around the issue of balance and find ways to ensure the relationship continued to contain them both happily.

As it was, changes to their being and doing—time for themselves, time together, and energy for themselves and together—resulted in a complex disturbance of their connection in terms of how they engaged with each other, and to their sense of agreement. This, essentially, was what lay behind the infidelity. While the hurt and trauma it left could not be simply wiped out, I was aware that as the balance in their communication changed, with David experiencing the value that can come from saying how he felt and Bree feeling less responsibility for voicing concerns, things would improve, and that they would have opportunities to rebuild their mutual understanding.

I feel sad thinking about the painful consequences that can arise when another area of life, such as work, is prioritised over relationships. I often think of how our attachments to one another form outside of our awareness and how sometimes the full importance and meaning of them only become clear to us when we are confronted by the loss of them.

Story Two

Mo and Leila

Our parenting styles are so different – should we separate?

The Background

Mo and Leila met through their jobs twenty years ago, when both were in their early thirties. Mo worked for an employment agency and Leila was a graphic designer, freelancing sometimes for Mo's agency.

Five years later they married and soon afterwards Mo left his job to start his own agency. Leila joined him, but after a year they decided that living and working together was 'too much' and she left. Mo, who sees himself as 'determined, hard-working and strong on structure,' saw his agency flourish. Leila, who described herself as 'buzzy and creative, an ideas person', decided to go freelance.

Though they agreed that they were 'very different,' they also had a lot in common and that 'we were a good balance for each other'. Both had experienced discrimination in the past: Mo as the son of ambitious immigrant parents from Pakistan, who worked hard to give him a private education, and Leila as someone brought up in the care system. 'It was go under or fight to survive,' she said. 'I wasn't going to let the system beat me. I worked hard and I got into art college. I knew that was my way out, but growing up that way did make a fighter of me.'

Twelve years ago their son Jay was born. It was a difficult birth and from the start, Mo said, Jay was 'a handful—never sleeping through the night, noisy and unable to sit still or concentrate.'

Jay's little sister Suki was born two years later, and in contrast she was 'an easy, calm child who just did as she was told.'

When Jay was eight and Suki was six, Mo and Leila decided to separate. The challenges of parenting Jay, and their very different parenting styles, had 'brought us to our knees'. Mo's constant efforts to 'impose rules' contrasted with Leila's 'hands-off, child-focused parenting', and the two of them argued constantly. Realising that this was affecting the children, they decided to part, the children remaining in the family home with Leila, with seeing Mo frequently.

For a while, things seemed to be settled; Jay was diagnosed with ADHD (Attention Deficit Hyperactivity Disorder) and he went to a new school where he was given a lot of support. Both Mo and Leila found his teachers to be, in Leila's words, 'brilliant with him and brilliant at keeping us informed'. In the process of the investigations into Jay's condition, both Mo and Leila recognised that Jay was 'more like his mum,' and that Leila had 'most of the symptoms of ADD (Attention Deficit Disorder), but without the hyperactivity.' Though she had no formal diagnosis, an online test confirmed their suspicion.

After two years apart, during which they were able to co-parent 'reasonably peacefully,' Mo and Leila decided to move back in together. 'We hated the family being apart, 'Leila said. 'We missed each other, the kids missed Mo, none of it felt right, so we decided to give it another go.'

For the next year things went well. Jay was settled in his school and was 'much easier' at home. The family had found peace. But when Jay was eleven, he had to leave his school and move on to secondary school. At that point 'all hell broke loose,' Mo said. 'The change to a much bigger school was too much for Jay' and he began, in Mo's words, 'acting up—playing loud music in the middle of the night, vandalising the neighbour's fence and arguing about absolutely everything'.
Once again, Mo and Leila began to argue. 'Mo told Jay what to do, he told me what to do, it drove me crazy,' Leila said. 'Now I'm wondering if we should separate again.'
'I wanted peace, and order,' Mo said miserably. 'I had Jay firing off in one direction and Leila firing off in the other and it was too much. But I don't want us to separate, I want us to find a way to work together.'

Their decision to come and see me was a 'last-ditch attempt to keep the family together' and to find a way through the 'parenting minefield'.

Towards the end of their second session with me, they mentioned that they were planning to build an extension onto their home, so that Jay could have a bigger room, further away from the rest of the family's bedrooms.

'I felt we'd all be able to breathe if we did it,' Mo said. 'But now that's turned into a minefield too.'

The session ended there.

My Initial Response

I notice that my reaction to news of the building project is ambivalent. The aim is to provide more space and some separation between Jay and the rest of the family, but I wonder about its meaning for Mo, Leila, Jay, and even Suki. I find myself thinking of the tension that always arises for us around how much we need to do when faced with a situation that feels uncomfortable, and I suspect that underneath the building project decision is the alienation that they feel in trying to think together about Jay.

In terms of their togethering, I think of this as a tension in their engaging: they are misunderstanding each other because of the way they approach thinking differently. Mo is someone who thinks silently and alone, while Leila thinks aloud and with others. As a result, it seems that Leila experiences Mo as someone who makes decisions without her, and therefore most likely feels excluded. Mo, on the other hand experiences Leila as overwhelming to the point where he cannot think. In simple terms, while they are in agreement about what matters, disagreement between them can come from undertaking a project together and they have yet to accept that fact.

In Session

'Can you tell me a bit more about the building project?' I ask.

Mo puts his head in his hands. 'It seemed like such a simple idea,' he says. 'I just wanted to get it costed and planned and to get it done over the school summer holidays.'But Leila and Jay keep coming up with new ideas for it, I can't pin anything down, and it's getting more complicated every day.'

'I just want it to be right,' Leila says, looking animated. 'I thought it could be soundproofed, so that Jay can make as much noise as he wants. And then I thought, why not add a little bathroom for him? And a door to the garden, so that he can come and go, when he's older. And Jay thought if the roof was flat there could be a little outside iron staircase up to it and he could make a garden there. He loves growing things.'

'A roof garden?' Mo says. 'Honestly, it's crazy. He'll fall off the roof on day one.'

'He won't, actually,' Leila says, glaring at him. 'We'll put a barrier round it. It will give him something that's all his own. He needs that.'

'What he needs is clear rules and consistency from us,' Mo says, 'not his own property empire at the back of the house. I just can't deal with the two of you bombarding me with your ideas and constantly changing things.'

'Oh, you're so stuck in your ways,' Leila huffs. 'And you don't give Jay a chance, you're always on his case, ordering him about, grounding him. Just because you were forced to fit in with your parents' expectations, doesn't mean our child has to be the same. Jay is a free spirit.'

'Is grounding him so unreasonable, given what he did to the neighbour's fence? You are the one who has got ADD and what with his ADHD someone around here has to try and keep a lid on things,' Mo says. 'He deserved it, and then two hours after I've told him he's grounded, you're undermining me, shouting at me that I can't do that. So then Jay starts shouting about his human rights and the whole thing is a madhouse.'

Leila points at Mo, her voice raised. 'I might have ADD but you're the mad one. I've honestly had enough of your trying to control everything. That's why I think we should separate again.'

Mo looks at her and then slumps back into his seat. 'I just don't know any more, I can't think, I've no idea . . .' he says.

Leila looks at him, surprised, and then looks at me.

'Hmmm,' I say, 'I don't think things are going well here.'

Leila sinks back down into her chair.

No one speaks. I feel there is something valuable in the silence, so I remain quiet.

Ten minutes later, neither Mo nor Leila has moved or spoken.

'It's time for us to end,' I say.

The Moment

For Leila and for Mo, the silence that followed my comment *I don't think things are going well here* was the moment of surrender, the point at which they stopped arguing and taking positions and shared the experience of stillness and silence that brought clarity and the potential for communion and ease.

What Happened Next

Two weeks later, Mo and Leila came for their next session. Both of them appeared relaxed and smiling.

'What happened after the last session?' I asked them.

'The children were with my sister, so we went for a quiet meal together,' Leila said. 'It did us both good, we stopped arguing and shouting and just talked. And we realised that the silence at the end of the session had felt good. It reminded us of something.'

She looked at Mo, who continued. 'It reminded us of when we were first going out together. We lived in Brighton, and we used to go down and sit on a bench above the beach. We'd sit for hours sometimes, holding hands and enjoying the view.'

'I looked at the clouds, mostly, the amazing shapes they made,' Leila laughed.

'I looked at the pier, its magnificent design and all the variety of life happening on it,' Mo said. 'So, we were in our different places but in the same place too. It was magical.'

Leila explained that after their last session and the dinner that followed, she had decided to contact a friend of theirs, an architect. Mo had actually suggested they contact him when the extension idea first cropped up, but Leila had thought it would be more fun to design it themselves.

'Mo was right though,' she said. 'We did need help. And Troy, our friend, was great. He said he'd designed something similar not long before. He came up with a plan and a costing we could manage and said it could be done over the summer.'

'He even got in most of the things Leila and Jay wanted,' Mo said. 'We agreed to drop the roof garden idea but to include the rest, including soundproofing which, given Jay's proclivities, is actually a really clever idea. It feels good to have it sorted. We're excited about it now.'

Leila smiled. 'We are,' she said.

'And Jay and Suki? How are they doing?' I ask.

'Suki is suddenly much more engaged. I hadn't really thought of her as being withdrawn but she is laughing, dancing, and singing in a way she hasn't for ages,' Mo says.

'And Jay is calmer and more relaxed, a bit like he was at his previous school,' Leila adds. 'I guess that with both of them I thought it was just change that came with age, but now I think they were unhappy because Mo and I were struggling.'

My Reflections

It is hard when partners united by ideals that come from difficult life experiences then find that their relationship has become a further place of pain as opposed to the place of care and safety they sought. Leila and Mo first came together through their beliefs around equality and their shared experience of discrimination, but they found that they had very different ways of being. This worked pretty well for them in general, but they struggled to find consensus around parenting Jay. While their very different ways of being worked for them in other areas of their lives, in this one key area they could not find a way through that both of them felt comfortable with.

Underpinning their frustration and conflict was a strong sense in both of them that they did not want to separate for a second time: they wanted to find a way through, together. Their love and appreciation for one another was evident. But despite this, the row over their parenting styles was circular, going back around the same cycle again and again and I felt sad that their resilience and courage was somehow being lost as they came to see each other as oppressors.

Sometimes, I find that the best intervention is the simplest, and that is to state what is happening in the room. So I said aloud what was evident—that things were not going well. This statement of the apparently obvious allowed them to pause.

They might have expected me to say something more, about what they could or could not do next, but my feeling was that there had been so many words spoken, and so many attempts to 'do', that a silent pause might be more productive.

A few minutes spent in silence can seem like a long time, but it can also bring relief and clarity. For Mo and Leila, it allowed a re-set; they were able to stop arguing and find a more constructive way forward. As is often the case, the prospect that something might be lost can be enough to make us stop and reevaluate.

The consensus they reached over the extension was significant—after so much disagreement they realised that they could find a way to work together and create an outcome that would benefit them and their children. It is so often the case that the business of living and the pressures that come with what needs doing can overshadow what really matters.

Story Three

Saul and Luciano

We can't stop having petty arguments

The Background
Saul and Luciano came for therapy because, having been together for about twelve years, they had become stuck in a vicious cycle of small arguments, as they described them. 'Petty arguments,' Saul said, which would result in 'painful standoffs in which we don't speak, or we're cool and distant with one another for several days at a time'. In the last couple of years, the arguments had become 'more and more frequent,' and that meant that the two of them ended up spending 'less time together, had less sex and fun and felt more stressed'.

'I simply don't feel supported,' Saul said.

'And neither do I,' Luciano added.

Luciano, who is Spanish, and Saul, who is British, met when they both went on a Gay Pride parade. They were each with their own groups of friends but, when there was an altercation with a couple of drunk men who shouted abuse from the sidelines, Luciano began to argue back, and it looked as though things might get very heated. At that point, Saul stepped in to calm things down, leading Luciano away from the drunks.

Once he'd cooled down, Luciano thanked Saul. He gave me a hug,' Saul said, which made the usually shy Saul 'blush with pleasure'. He added, 'We laughed together like drunken idiots, got talking, exchanged numbers and agreed to meet up that evening.'

From that time onwards they were together, their joyous relationship based around shared values of freedom of expression and rights, and their deeply held beliefs about equality and peace.

Five years ago, things changed when Luciano began to work longer hours in his job running a care agency, and they began to have less free time together. The trigger for Luciano was 'the referendum on Britain's membership of the European Union. It made me feel very insecure.' Growing up in Spain, in a religious family, he had not felt that his sexuality was accepted. After moving to Britain he found 'acceptance and love'.

'Then suddenly, my whole way of life seemed to be threatened.' He decided to work hard, so that he could save enough money to support him and Saul in either Britain or Spain.

Two years ago, Luciano proposed to Saul. 'I felt that this would be a way to ensure I could stay in Britain, but I didn't say this to Saul, as it seemed so unromantic. And the more I thought about us marrying, the more excited I got. I ended up planning a romantic meal in the restaurant where we had our first date, and I proposed over a glass of champagne. I felt it would seal our love and it would help me too, so the best of both worlds.'

When Saul turned the proposal down, Luciano was 'absolutely gutted'. For his part, Saul was astonished that Luciano had proposed. 'I felt that marriage would be conforming to oppressive social values that Luciano and I don't believe in.'

Saul felt that 'romantic as the proposal was, we would regret marrying'.

It was around that time that they began to argue more often. Saul felt 'depressed' about the state of their relationship and eventually they agreed that they would go to therapy together.

In the first session, both Saul and Luciano talked about how they saw theirs as a really 'strong relationship'. Both were committed to finding 'a way through our problems'.

In the second session, we agreed to start looking in more detail at what was happening during their conflicts.

My Initial Response

When I heard about Luciano's proposal and Saul's refusal I felt shocked and sad. And as always, when I feel something in response to what partners are saying, it raises the question: *Does this feeling of mine have the potential to be of service here?* To answer this question, I had to reflect on several things, including my own experiences of rejection, what I know professionally about rejection, how the information was shared, and the dynamic between Luciano and Saul.

I concluded that my shock was not about my own experiences of rejection, but rather it was an alert to the shock for their relationship, which had suffered a wound or trauma that might well have the power to destabilise it. The story of the proposal left me with many questions and I suspected that this was because they were themselves unclear about how this could have happened for them.

I was certain that Luciano's experience of a sense of threat to his security following the EU referendum result had not been fully understood by either of them. I was moved in thinking about Luciano's insecurity, and also what I suspected to be Saul's loneliness.

I thought of communion in terms of the moment of their meeting, and of ease through the period prior to the referendum. Conversely, I thought about a sense of unease following the referendum and then alienation at the moment of the proposal.

I noticed Luciano's response to his unease was to look to two particular pillars of life to help counter his insecurity: he focused on work and he thought, in practical terms, about how to secure his relationship.

I suspected the balance of their togethering was disturbed, firstly through their having less time together, and also by misunderstandings because of an apparent divergence in their doing and agreeing, with Saul feeling the greater burden of the domestic chores and the creeping erosion of trust in shared values and equality.

Finally, their engaging was not enabling them to form a shared understanding of these impacts. They both seemed to be striving in their differing ways without agreeing on it together, preventing them from understanding that they were both desperate for the same thing—the return of how they used to experience their relationship.

In Session
'We had an argument again last night, one of those petty little arguments, and I've been so upset, I've just not been able to speak about it,' Saul says.

I say, 'so last night was one of the arguments that we spoke about in the first session? The kind of argument that the two of you have struggled with?'

'Yes,' they both reply.

'I'm wondering what the argument was about,' I say.

'Ha!' says Saul, 'talking about conforming to other people's relationship expectations, it was about putting out the rubbish. You see, I end up doing all the planning stuff around the house, you know? All the practical things. I do the weekly shop online, I sort out the bills, I organise the cleaner, I do the washing .

'Is that a problem?' I ask.

'I like doing all that stuff,' Saul says. 'Don't get me wrong. I mean I like looking after our home and keeping it nice. But I feel a little uncomfortable because, well, going back to the societal thing, then, you know, it's a bit like, I end up being the one at home, the "wife" having to sort out the stuff while the "husband" is busy working; the kind of thing that was the norm in the 1950s. So, there is a bit of discomfort around that.

'There's just one thing that I always ask Luciano to do, and that is put the rubbish out. And, as usual, last night, he forgot. Well, he said forgot, but he always forgets. So, for me, it's not just that he's forgotten, it's that he doesn't want to do it. And then I get really frustrated because he's agreed to do it, he says he wants to do it, but he doesn't do it. I think he doesn't want to do it. And it just really annoys me that he can't be honest about it.'

'OK,' I say. 'Luciano, what would you like to say about this?'

'I really appreciate all the work that Saul does, I do. And I do want to put the rubbish out and do my bit. But I work so hard, I'm always on my emails, there's a project that I'm working on, and there's so much I'm involved in that I forget about other stuff. Saul is so organised, he plans everything; he remembers all the birthdays, he pays all the bills on time. I forget about all these things. Saul will turn his emails off at five o'clock at night. I can't do that; I'm looking at my emails at 10 o'clock at night. As something comes in I'm straight on to it. I wish I wasn't so busy, but I am, and I can't sleep unless everything is cleared. I need to make sure that everything gets sorted out before I can relax.'

I notice in myself a feeling of exhaustion and misery and the thought pops into my head: *I could do with a laugh right now*. As this occurs to me, I wonder about the fun in their relationship.

'I'm thinking that it sounds as though life became very serious for the two of you some time ago,' I say. 'Do you have fun together nowadays?'

They shift in their seats and Saul says, 'Well, we haven't had a holiday for a year. We do meet up with friends and things but yeah, we don't play together much. And we hardly ever have sex nowadays. I miss what we used to be like before things got so heavy. Luciano talks about being afraid of us being separated but quite often I feel lonely. It's as though we've already been separated, even though we're still together.'

Luciano starts to cry, gently at first but then there are deep sobs.

Saul looks over at Luciano and says, 'What's wrong? Why are you so upset? What's going on?'

Luciano continues to sob. After a little while he seems to regain some composure. He dries his eyes and then he says, 'I am just feeling so sad. I've spent the last five years desperately trying to keep us together and all my efforts have just kept us apart. I miss us too. I miss you, Saul. I miss how much fun we used to have.'

Saul moves close to Luciano and puts his arm around him and hugs him. We sit in silence for a minute or so and then Luciano turns to look into Saul's eyes. His look is concerned and caring. Suddenly Luciano gives Saul a little poke in the ribs and they both begin to laugh.

The Moment

My intervention came when my feeling of exhaustion led to my thinking about the opposite of what Saul and Luciano were speaking about: as they discussed chores, I wondered about fun. The whole energy of the relationship had, over time, become skewed towards the practical tasks of living and the admin of being in a relationship. Being alerted to something that had become hidden from them acted to break their pattern of focus and to allow them to reconnect.

When both of them dissolve into laughter, recognising the struggles both had gone through and that behind those struggles was their deep their love for one another, it was the moment of understanding for Saul and Luciano, one of communion as they shifted into a state of *ataraxy*.

What Happened Next

After the breakthrough, Luciano started to make more time for fun. As he did so, his anxiety diminished and so did Saul's. Luciano continued to work as hard as before and Saul continued to take care of the household, but they made sure that there were times when they could have fun. They even made some household chores into games they could play, for instance racing to put the bins out and hiding them from one another.

A few months later, they entered into a civil partnership, which brought both of them peace of mind in terms of their shared future in Britain. Luciano now has British citizenship, which he is delighted about, and Saul is going to apply for Spanish citizenship. Curiously, they also found that after their civil partnership they felt more relaxed and secure. They agreed that, to their surprise, the civil partnership, which they had thought of as an instrument of oppression, actually brought them security and liberation.

My Reflection

Saul did not reject Luciano's proposal because it was the wrong solution, but because the proposal had different meanings for each of them and they hadn't jointly arrived at the proposal as the solution to the issue of Luciano's insecurity. Relationships often struggle because there is a lack of clarity around what the partners expect will be decided between them, in other words, where they will agree, or have consensus.

Additionally, for Luciano and Saul, the proposal was clearly at odds with the belief system on which their relationship rested. In heterosexual relationships a proposal is something that happens due to expectations driven by society. In a nonheterosexual relationship, those expectations are much less likely to exist, as society has less influence.

In the wake of the rupture to their relationship caused by the proposal and its rejection, their togethering was affected in being and doing. As the cycle of arguments began, they had less time together, less energy available for each other, and growing levels of misunderstanding in both their verbal and non-verbal communication. All of this resulted in less agreeing or consensus around the day-to-day aspects of keeping a relationship in balance.

As is so often the case, their 'petty little argument' was not about the apparent issue—the bins—but about the underlying struggle that was putting pressure on the balance of their relationship. The underlying struggle was the unease that had come into their relationship around the issue of support. Saul's reaction to the proposal meant Luciano felt unsupported and, as work became more important to Luciano as a source of support and security, his focus changed and he forgot to put the bins out, which meant that Saul also felt unsupported.

What Saul and Luciano had missed was the opportunity to talk about why Luciano had proposed. In the shock of the situation Saul didn't ask Luciano about why he had arrived at that decision, and Luciano didn't explain that it was connected to his anxiety about staying in Britain.

In presenting his solution to Saul Luciano neglected to provide his reasoning, which meant that his struggle was not understood. After the rejection, feeling hurt and in the light of their differing opinions, Luciano accepted responsibility for dealing with his anxiety alone, rather than sharing the problem.

It is often the case that, as in Saul and Luciano's situation, partners become so focused on the serious aspects of their relationship that they lose sight of the fun. These two things are on the same continuum, and I often find myself saying to people in a situation like this: 'When we are looking left, we are not looking right.'

Story Four

Richard and Ellie

Her parents are so controlling

The Background

Richard and Ellie had been together for five years, and in therapy with me for one. Early on in our sessions, they talked about how they met: Richard began talking to Ellie at a party and then invited her to go out with him for a drink a few days later.

'I spotted her across the room,' Richard said. 'I thought she was gorgeous, but I was nervous because I can be a bit full-on, and I didn't want to put her off.'

'And I was nervous because I can hold back, people can find me a bit quiet,' Ellie said. 'I'm always worried that they will think I'm uninteresting.'

'I certainly didn't,' Richard smiled. 'I thought you were lovely.'

They both laughed at the worries they'd had initially. 'The truth was we just clicked and that was it,' Ellie said. They happily agreed that Richard did the choosing and Ellie was chosen. They both felt this has been a good dynamic for them: they have a fairly harmonious relationship in which they seldom argue, and they feel that they balance one another out.

They decided to come to therapy for reassurance. When we talked about it, Richard used the analogy of stabilisers on a bicycle, and Ellie agreed with this. They wanted to know that when problems arose, they would know how to deal with them.

'I often feel a sense of security and contentment, but I can suddenly feel anxious,' Ellie said. 'I think we understand each other and fit well together but then I think, "are we doing something wrong?"'

Richard nods in agreement.

'Can I ask about reassurance?' I ask them during the discussion. 'Is that something particular to one of you, or both of you?'

Richard replied, 'I tend not to feel a need for reassurance outside the relationship.'

Ellie said, 'I do tend to need reassurance generally.'

In the time they have been seeing me, Ellie has switched jobs from office work to teacher training, and they have moved home after buying a flat together. They have managed both these life changes without too much difficulty. But one issue did arise. When we discussed their families, both felt that Ellie's parents were 'very controlling,' and that Ellie had 'difficulty standing up to them'. This had been a source of some friction between the two of them. In particular, a discussion about Christmas in our last session, revealed some areas of disagreement.

'Ellie's mother has health problems,' Richard said. 'She uses this as a way to insist that we spend several days over Christmas with her and Ellie's father every year. Ellie feels unable to say no to her mother, who tells her, every year, that this could be her last Christmas.'

Richard feels that it's 'unfair' that they never see his parents at Christmas.

We had agreed to discuss this in our next session, but unfortunately, due to a family emergency, I was unable to make it. I sent a message cancelling, but Richard and Ellie didn't see it, so they turned up for the session.

The next time they came to see me, I found myself wondering how they would be with me. I had been thinking about ruptures in therapy and about how there's never a mistake, only material to work with. In other words, I had been nervous, and looked at concepts and experiences to reassure myself and bring some useful thoughts to share with Richard and Ellie.

My Initial Response

I warmed instantly to Richard and Ellie and my experience of meeting them resulted in feelings I understood as 'parental'. This is not unusual: I tend to think of my role as a therapist as sometimes being about performing a parental role, as I am there to get my clients to the point when they no longer need me. When I take on clients, we agree a structure for our meetings, our togethering, in terms of time, duration and cost, all of which need to be optimal. This allows for a clarity against which the source of misunderstandings or confusion can be revealed.

I wanted to understand their need for reassurance and also what it was that they found reassuring. In practice, this meant asking them what they were getting from sessions, what they found helpful, and not so helpful. As is often the case, I notice that my acceptance of what people tell me they find helpful or unhelpful is crucial, because often children are told what should be helpful and unhelpful rather than being given the time and space to determine this for themselves.

In my warmth towards both Richard and Ellie was founded on a belief in them: I was certain that they just needed to get to a point of being able to reassure themselves.

In Session
As I meet Richard and Ellie at the door, their greeting is as friendly as ever, but I am aware that there is some additional energy around them.

When we go into the therapy room and take our seats, I expect a pause before one of them speaks, as is usual, but this time Richard launches straight in.

'Was everything okay with your family in the end?' he asks.

'Yes,' I reply. 'Thank you. It was a difficult situation and I'm sorry I had to cancel at short notice. How was it for you when you turned up to find that I wasn't here?'

'Well,' Richard smiles broadly, 'actually, we have some news. I am very excited, and I think you are too Ellie, right?'

Ellie nods and laughs. 'Yes, I am.'

'Do you want to tell him or shall I?' Richard says.

Ellie nudges him. 'You start.'

'We've decided we can start to wind up our sessions with you,' Richard says.

'Don't worry, we're not angry or upset with you. Quite the opposite,' Ellie adds.

'I'm intrigued,' I say. 'Would you like to tell me what happened?'

'At first we were shocked when we realised you weren't here,' Richard says. 'I felt quite upset because I had a lot of things I wanted us to talk about, like the Christmas issue with Ellie's mum, which we said we'd discuss. So I was a bit poleaxed. But then I had an idea and I said to Ellie, "Why don't we go and sit in the park and use the time to talk, just the two of us?"'

'I wasn't sure at first,' Ellie says. 'We've relied on our time with you quite a lot when we've needed to sort something out between us. But then I had the sudden thought that there was a time before therapy when we were great together and that recently things have been moving in the right direction and I knew Richard was right.'

'So how did that go?' I ask.

'It was a bit of an odd experience,' Ellie says. 'It was as though we were trying to have a session imagining you there. I said to Richard if we got stuck, we could just ask ourselves "What would Nicholas say or do now?"'

'We started talking about the Christmas thing and Ellie's mum and instead of both of us getting tense and miserable as we have in the past, we worked it out,' Richard says. 'It took us a while, we talked for the whole hour, and in the end we both felt we had got somewhere. We decided . . . well, Ellie, you tell him,' he says, turning to her.

She smiles at him. 'We agreed that I would ring Mum and tell her that we can only come to her and Dad for Christmas Eve and that after that we're going to see Richard's parents on Christmas Day this year.'

'You both sound really pleased,' I say. 'You two make a good team, you work well together.'

'Yes,' Richard says. 'By the time we left the park we felt as though we could work something difficult out on our own and reach a compromise.'

'So, by the end of your park session you had decided you were ready to wind down the therapy?' I ask.

They both laugh.

'It's as if you not being there was the stabilisers on the bike breaking,' Richard says. 'And then we found we could ride the bike without them.'

The Moment

For Richard and Ellie, the moment in which they reached understanding happened when they were not with me, and for me it was a pleasure to hear them describe it.

When Richard said they were shocked that I wasn't there, and then they decided to go to the park and talk, that was the point when things shifted, as they went from feeling they needed me to realising that they could manage without me.

What Happened Next

Richard and Ellie came to see me twice more, to wind down and then end their therapy. In those sessions there was a lot of laughter, and I was conscious of a sense of release and of achievement in both of them. They had always been a well-balanced team, but now they knew that, and it was clear that it felt good.

They followed through with their decision about Christmas, and in our last session they told me about it.

'I was very nervous,' Ellie admitted. 'But Richard sat with me while I made the call, and I did it. I told Mum I loved her, but that we needed to see Richard's parents too.'

'How did that go? 'I asked.

Ellie smiled. 'Do you know, she accepted it. I had expected a meltdown: there have been so many of those in the past. But I think she knew that this time I meant it. She was grumpy, but I could handle that.'

'I was proud of Ellie,' Richard said. 'Her mum can be a bit of a tyrant, but Ellie didn't get caught up in the usual stuff, she stuck to what we had agreed.'

As they said goodbye at the end of that last session, I sensed the calm and the confidence between them.

A year after I last saw them Richard and Ellie sent me a card, telling me that they were planning to get married, and that Ellie was expecting a baby.

My Reflections

In the sessions with Richard and Ellie we had a pattern of looking at concerns: they would tell me where they had got to, I would ask some questions that would deepen their conversations and then they would leave saying that they felt reassured.

For them their 'togethering' was impacted through the degree to which they generally had agreement, or consensus, and they ended up uneasy that things between them seemed so easy. The cost of such uneasiness was the impact it had being able to experience moments of communion, and hence the need for reassurance—in Ellie's case generally, and in Richard's specifically within the relationship.

The judgment that Ellie's parents were 'controlling ' suggests that the parents were unclear about who they needed to be for Ellie. Often, the relationship between parents and their children is, or becomes, confused, so that rather than the parents' objective of being there to bring the child to independence in adulthood, there is a dependency or dynamic that prevents a comfortable separation. Although it was the relationship between Ellie and Richard that was brought to therapy, the outcome was actually to address the probable source of Ellie's and therefore the relationship's need for reassurance—the need for Ellie to navigate a new way of relating to her parents.

After I had missed their session, I felt conscious that my message hadn't reached them, and I wondered how they might feel about it. But these things happen—in therapy as in life—and while it could have been a difficult situation ('things going wrong,') it turned out on this occasion to be the catalyst for positive change. My unexpected absence, after a period of my dependable presence, turned out to be pivotal in Richard and Ellie's move to independence.

Story Five

Vicky and Angus

I'm afraid she is becoming an alcoholic

The Background

Vicky and Angus began therapy in the autumn of 2020. They said they had been 'arguing about her drinking' and they felt their relationship was 'in trouble'. Angus was 'worried' about Vicky's alcohol intake, which he said 'had increased significantly in the previous few months,' while Vicky found Angus 'annoying' and wished he would 'just leave her alone'.

Vicky had started her own company a few years earlier, catering for events such as festivals, weddings, and concerts. She worked hard and did well and within a few months she was able to take on an assistant, and then a second one.

Angus had been working as an accountant, but he didn't enjoy his job and when Vicky's business began to grow and she was bringing in enough money to support the family, they agreed that he should become a stay-at-home dad, looking after their two daughters, aged eight and ten.

Both Vicky and Angus were happy with this set-up: she said that she 'loved being my own boss', while he said he was 'enjoying having more time with the children'. Then came the pandemic and almost overnight, as the events she catered for were all cancelled, Vicky's business collapsed. She had to put her two staff members on furlough.

Vicky talked about feeling herself to be 'responsible for supporting the family'. She said that while she had always enjoyed a glass of wine in the evening, she had begun to 'drink a lot more'.

When they tried to talk about what was happening, Vicky would say she was 'anxious and depressed' and Angus would respond with 'you don't need to be', but both said they still 'felt stuck' and that talking 'wasn't helping'.

When they came for therapy, we talked about how they were as individuals. The dynamic Vicky and Angus described was that she would usually be 'proactive and step straight into taking action', while Angus was 'quieter and more reserved' and would often 'step back, observing a situation before deciding whether to act or not'. This was reflected in their parenting styles. For instance, Vicky would insist their girls tidy their rooms regularly, while Angus would allow the girls more leeway in the way they kept their rooms and would discuss it with them.

In general, they said, the dynamic between them had worked well. However, since Vicky had lost her business, Angus had become increasingly alarmed and worried at the change in her. She seemed to be 'doing more and more' and he increasingly felt 'powerless'. It seemed that their differences were becoming amplified over time. He had been reluctant to step in, knowing that she already 'felt bad' and concerned that she would feel 'criticised or undermined', but he began to feel that he was 'struggling to cope with the situation'. When he did, finally, bring up his worries about her drinking, telling her that he was 'afraid she was becoming an alcoholic', she had at first been 'defensive' but had eventually begun to cry and admitted that she felt 'enormous pressure'. Angus had suggested therapy and Vicky had, reluctantly, agreed.

Although initially we spoke about Vicky's drinking, the discussion soon shifted to her business collapse and her anxiety about it. Vicky said she felt that she had 'let the family down', even though she couldn't have foreseen the pandemic or the effect it would have on her business. She felt very worried about the family's lack of income and was afraid they would lose their home if they couldn't pay the mortgage. This was linked to intrusive memories from her childhood, when her father had lost his job and the family had moved into a much smaller home.

My Initial Response

I felt a sense of communion with Vicky when we talked about her work and her enjoyment of getting things done, while with Angus, our connection was strongest in talking about times of peace and tranquility. I thought about the amount of change that they had both individually experienced and how that had impacted their togethering; certainly there was less time together. I suspected a change in energy and something around the way their engaging with each other meant that they were not really able to agree.

The word that came to my mind to capture Angus's experience was *impotence*, given the apparent power of the alcohol, and I thought about how this seemed so similar to Vicky's sense of powerlessness. I was certain that Angus and Vicky needed to get back to a place where their differing strengths balanced the relationship. As often happens for me, an image came to mind, and I thought of a tug of war. I imagined Vicky having been able to pull Angus, but in my fantasy Angus didn't pull Vicky back towards him: instead they both let go of the rope and walked towards each other. I saw that as a potential moment for communion and a return to ease.

In Session

'I'm just so afraid about the future,' Vicky says. 'I feel what happened to my family when I was twelve is happening all over again. When we had to move into a smaller flat my dad started drinking. It affected all of us badly.'

'Do you feel that the same thing is happening now, and that you are like your dad?' I ask.

'No, I'm *nothing* like him,' she says, with emphasis. 'Dad was a heavy drinker and we were frightened of him.'

I turn to Angus, who is looking perplexed. 'What's going on for you?' I ask him.

He hesitates then glances at Vicky. 'I don't feel frightened of you,' he says. 'But I do feel frightened to talk to you about your drinking.'

Vicky looks startled and then becomes tearful. I pass her the tissues.

'I understand how worried you are after what happened when you were young,' Angus continues. 'But really you don't need to worry so much, we're not in the same situation your dad was in.'

'In what way is it different?' I ask. 'Do you have financial difficulties?'

'No,' Angus says. 'We don't. We have a good amount saved. It will last us for a couple of years if we need it to. And we haven't even dipped into our savings yet because Vicky got a couple of government grants to keep the business going.
'And there's another thing—I can get a job. I'm a qualified accountant and there are always jobs going, so if I have to, I'll go back to work.'

'Ah,' I say. 'That's interesting. Vicky, what do you think about that?'

Vicky is looking from me to Angus and back, and she looks as though she has just heard something that is new to her.

'Well, I suppose Angus is right,' she says, wiping her eyes. 'I'm so used to being anxious about money, I never think we've got enough, I always feel disaster is around the next corner.'

'I'm so sorry,' Angus says to her. 'It must be painful feeling that way. I wish I'd said something sooner, but I didn't realise I needed to. And I felt somehow that I wasn't . . . entitled to question things. I was afraid that if I interfered you might feel I was making things worse, I thought holding back was the best thing I could do for you.'

Vicky laughs through her tears. 'I had no idea you felt like that. I really wanted you to do something, or say something, but I don't think I even realised it myself. I've been feeling so alone. The last thing I want is you to be frightened of talking to me.'

'You're not alone,' Angus says. 'We're in this together. We'll cope with the situation together.'

The shift in Vicky at this point is visible: her face softens, her shoulders, which had been hunched, are lowered, and she smiles. Beside her, Angus smiles too, as he takes her hand.

The Moment

For Vicky and Angus, the moment of revelation was when I asked them if they had financial difficulties. Hearing that Angus was not anxious and hearing him outline their financial security brought Vicky's own anxiety into clearer focus. It was also important for her to hear Angus say that he was qualified and could get a job. In saying this, her feelings of being solely responsible for the family finances were challenged.

Vicky's family background and the losses her family suffered when she was a child were the source of the fear she felt around money: Angus, who came from a financially stable family, felt far less concern about it. They had misunderstood what was important to each other.

What Happened Next
Going forward, I asked Vicky and Angus to make an explicit agreement with one another: that Angus would step in if he saw Vicky behaving in a way that he believed was driven by anxiety. For instance, if she said she needed to work on a Sunday—a sign that they both told me had, in the past, led to her feeling stressed and tired and to arguments between them— Angus could say something like, 'Hold on, we need to talk about this.'

Vicky, for her part, agreed that she would listen when he challenged her in this way, and that she would step back sometimes, to decelerate and take a little time out. She also agreed to challenge Angus if she felt that he was taking too much of a back seat. Their agreement was to challenge and be challenged. An agreement like this can only work if both take part, and they were both keen to do this.

Vicky and Angus needed to recognise that their different styles—her stepping in and his stepping back—are equally valid and equally powerful and that they can achieve the best balance when they are both involved.

Their agreement worked well. Over the next few months they both reported that things felt much better. Vicky started her business again, sending out food hampers, and as things began to open up in the summer of 2021 and, after a winter of lockdown, she had a flood of wedding catering orders. With her business back on its feet her confidence and her income returned. Angus was happy to continue to be the at-home parent, but he also took on the accounting side of the business, so that he could give Vicky more visible support.

When, in the last session, I pointed out that when they had first arrived, they had spoken about drinking, but that we had not talked about that any more, they laughed. 'It was never really about the drinking,' Angus said.

My Reflections

When the word 'alcoholic' is used it is highly charged and emotive and it will have a profound effect on both the user and the person they are addressing. For this reason, it can be counter-productive to use a label: instead of opening up the conversation it can close it down or take it in the direction of conflict.

When I am working with people, I think less about the behaviour that is being raised as the issue and more about the cause of the behaviour. With Vicky and Angus I wondered, 'What is it that alcohol is actually bringing Vicky?'

Angus and Vicky cope with pressure in different ways—under pressure Vicky is likely to do more and Angus is likely to do less. And this will be true in all aspects of their lives. Neither reaction to pressure is better or worse than the other, although it is likely that each may feel disquieted by the other one's way of coping and might feel that the other 'should' be doing either more or less.

Their different approaches to pressure need not be a problem: they can balance one another well. It only becomes a problem when they are not engaging effectively and sharing their experiences. In the absence of a joint understanding, they can very easily exhaust each other.

Alcohol will further complicate the situation—it is a substance that alters mood and behaviour and so the effects of alcohol will mean that your experience might be that you are dealing with two different people. The person who has increased their drinking becomes unrecognisable in all aspects of togethering: being, doing, engaging, and agreeing.

For Vicky and Angus, talking about their different reactions to pressure is important. And, as their respective ways of coping are a fine balance with one another, it can be really useful if they are able to challenge each other and—even more importantly— if they want to be challenged by one another: the agreement to needs to be active and explicit. We all of us grow up being criticised and monitored, and measured, so it's natural to find feedback from others difficult. When we are expecting it and we welcome it, it is much easier to receive and it's also easier to give.

In the light of this, I tell people at the start of our work together that if I have an opinion, I will share it. When I do have an opinion or a suggestion, or a view, I will then ask the person, or people, if they want to receive it. So far, no one has ever said *no*, but the request ensures that they are not taken by surprise.

Story Six

Sarah and Jackie

We aren't having enough sex

The Background
Both teachers in their late forties, Sarah and Jackie met at a conference seven years ago, and within a year they had moved in together.

Sarah is a physics teacher, while Jackie teaches drama, and both agree that they share 'a passion for knowledge and for the value of education'.

The difference in their subject areas reflects, in some ways, their different ways of being. Sarah is the 'quieter' of the two: she enjoyed focusing on gaining her master's degree, she finds socialising 'draining' and prefers a 'quiet night at home with Jackie'. For her part, Jackie likes to be involved in a 'variety of projects and activities' and she feels 'energised' when she spends time with others.

Both agreed that, despite their different ways of being, they felt very compatible, but recently Sarah had begun to feel that they were seeing 'less and less of one another' and this had led to their decision to come for therapy. When they arrived to see me for the first time, they told me that Sarah had prompted the decision and that Jackie had agreed in order to 'please Sarah'.

'We used to do more together,' Sarah said. 'But these days Jackie is always out and always busy. She goes to Pilates, to choir, and to a book club and I sit at home feeling sad because I miss her and wonder if there's something wrong with me because I don't do all those things. For me a long day at school is enough. I want to unwind, listen to some music, enjoy a nice meal and a glass of wine and spend time with the woman I love.'

Jackie said that she had 'never wanted to hurt Sarah' and she was dismayed to learn how much Sarah minded her being out several evenings a week. 'I love all the things I go to,' she said. 'I like meeting people and getting involved in activities. I don't get home late, and I tell Sarah all about what I've been doing. I can't change who I am, I'd just get bored spending every evening at home.'

'You didn't used to,' Sarah reminded her. 'When we first got together we spent all our spare time together. We had a very passionate relationship; we were so into each other. Now I feel it's more like a domestic arrangement, we have everything organised—our home, money and so on—but at times I feel we're just two people coexisting in the same house. I don't feel appreciated or wanted and that hurts.'

Jackie also said that she no longer felt appreciated by Sarah. 'When I'm out with other people I don't feel I'm being judged and found wanting all the time, or being asked to be someone different.'

My Initial Response

I noticed feelings that make sense to me through the word *de-skilled*, and this leads me to think about how both Jackie and Sarah are teachers with a passion for learning. I suspect that coming to see me is very difficult because they are both used to being able to find ways forward.

It was easy to see that the *being* element of togethering was suffering as they were gradually spending less time together. I was alerted by the word *passionate*, and I wondered about whether there was a change of energy or whether their sexual relationship had struggled to mature. I thought about the possibility of a struggle to be comfortable and agree on what happens sexually.

I was aware of the potential for Sarah, in particular, to be holding some feelings of shame around sex, because she talked about reduced passion as a symptom of their relationship struggle and Jackie's increasing activity outside the relationship as the cause. As is often the case the right things were talked about, but importance was placed on the wrong things. When this happens, it is often due to discomfort or shame around the existence of particular feelings and needs.

In Session

'You mentioned that you used to have a very passionate relationship,' I say. 'What is different now?'

This prompts a change in Sarah, who leans forward. 'Our sex life is almost non-existent,' she says, angrily. 'At our age most people are having sex at least a couple of times a week. For us it's more like once a month . . . if I'm lucky.'

'You're always spouting ridiculous statistics,' Jackie snaps back. 'But people are different. I can't help it if I don't want sex as much as you do.'

'So, there is a difference in desire? Are you both certain that this is not about health or bodily changes?' I ask.

'Yes,' Jackie says. 'After one of our previous arguments we ended up thinking one or both of us might be starting the menopause or have something else going on, so we did both go to see our GPs and everything was fine.'

'Okay, so it *is* about desire,' I say. 'Sarah, you would like more sex, and Jackie, you're happy with less?'

'That's right,' Jackie says. 'We're just different.'

'Sarah, I wonder what you think about Jackie saying that you are both different?'

'I find it really uncomfortable talking about this with a virtual stranger,' Sarah says, fiddling with a tissue.

'I'm sorry to hear you are feeling uncomfortable,' I say.

Sarah is paying close attention to me. 'Why are you asking?' she says.

'I do find that it's good to be able to talk about sex in the context of the relationship,' I explain. 'Often the dynamic in intimacy can shine a light on what is happening elsewhere. Perhaps the difference you both feel in levels of desire around sex is reflected in other parts of your relationship, such as the amount of time you spend together?'

'Hmm, well it was me who suggested therapy, so I suppose there's not much point if I'm not happy speaking about this,' Sarah says. 'It is true that I tend to prefer to focus more on fewer things whereas Jackie seems to prefer doing lots of different things but at less depth.'

'Yes I think that's right,' Jackie says, slowly. 'When it comes to sex, I orgasm after a short period of time and am happy to stop whereas Sarah . . .'

'I would like to have sex for hours,' Sarah interjects.

'So it does sound as though in sex, as with other time together, there is always a tension around how much feels good for both of you,' I say. 'I'm thinking that in the past this was tolerable, somehow. So perhaps it would be helpful to look at how things might have changed for you both?'

'They've definitely changed,' Sarah says, sounding bitter. 'We had a good sex life for the first few years, but it's just fizzled out.'

'Ha,' says Jackie, 'you say that, but you've always wanted more sex than I do. Anyway, you seem to be managing all right on your own.'

Sarah reddens. 'That's not fair,' she mutters.

There's a pause and Jackie looks at me.

'I walked in on Sarah having solo sex,' Jackie says. 'We ended up having a row and we haven't really talked about it since.'

'It was embarrassing,' Sarah says. 'What does she expect when we hardly ever have sex?'

'I am sorry to hear you felt embarrassed, Sarah,' I say. 'Can you say what thoughts came up for you when you felt the embarrassment?'

'I thought I was a bad person and that I was doing something I shouldn't be doing.'

'Oh no, I can't bear that you might think that way,' Jackie says, looking upset. 'When I walked in I was initially surprised and then, I suppose, in a way I felt guilty because I hadn't wanted to think about you not feeling fully sexually satisfied.'

She paused and then went on. 'The trouble is I feel that with sex, and with all the other things I like to do, it's as though you want me to change, but I'm not asking you to change, I'm just asking you to accept who I am and that when I don't feel like sex, I'm going to say no.'

'So, you fell in love in great part because you recognise and value each other's different ways of approaching life, but now you each want the other to change, to be more like you?' I say.

'Mmmm, I hadn't thought of it that way, but I suppose I do,' Jackie suddenly laughs. 'Look at me getting on my high horse and now I find I'm doing the same thing I've been accusing you of.'

She looks at Sarah, who says, 'I love how you can engage with so many different people and issues, the number of times you have encouraged me to do new things, and at others pointed out how I seem to be spending time on something I'm not really enjoying. I am so grateful to you for that.'

'Well,' Jackie replies, 'I remember the time I was taking my extra qualification and I got bored and wanted to give up and you were great, you said to me, "Look, you have one last paper to write, let me sit here with you," and you sat next to me. You didn't do or say anything; just you being there got me through. Looking back, it would have been awful if I had given up and I really admire how you can stick at things—including sticking with me.'

And they both laugh.

The Moment

For Jackie and Sarah, the moment of understanding came after I pointed out that they fell in love because they valued one another's different approaches to life. It was as if they had forgotten that the qualities they admired in each other were the exact same ones that had become the focus for their dissatisfaction. Once they both recognised this it reminded them of all the differences they loved in one another.

What Happened Next

Sarah and Jackie talked about the way the focus, for both of them, had shifted over time from feeling happy together to wanting the other to be different. Both were asking the other to do what they didn't want to do themselves—that is, to change. Accepting this allowed them to move forward.

The conversation about sex highlighted the way they could misinterpret one another's reactions and misunderstand each other. Once judgment and fear of judgment were removed, they were able to discuss the fact that not all sex in a relationship needs to happen for the couple together and that they might enjoy sex differently together.

This realisation became one of the aspects of their sex lives that helped them to find a compromise. Sarah again felt free to have solo sex if she wished, and as the discussion between them about intimacy became more open and they began to feel closer, they began to have sex more often. Not, perhaps, as often as Sarah wanted, but more often than had been the case for some time. They reached a compromise that both could happily accept, just as they had when they first met.

They also realised that there were more options available for them in what they did sexually. Jackie's interest in new things led to the introduction of sex toys and role-play, increasing the amount of time they spent having sex.

Sarah and Jackie also began to spend more time together. Sarah joined Jackie's book club and Jackie made a point of spending several evenings a week at home, cooking dinner together. Their sense of intimacy and connectedness was not the same as it had been earlier in their relationship; it was, as Sarah put it, 'less passionate but more ummm . . . well just that —*more*.'

My Reflections

For Sarah and Jackie, the key issue in their togethering was time. They could not agree on how much time to spend together, and although Sarah appeared to be the one most deeply troubled by that, it actually affected them both equally because it led to a lack of consensus between them around that area.

There was also a second issue troubling them both: their different levels of energy, which was experienced most poignantly through differences in their sexuality and the way that affected their desire. This lack of active agreeing was causing discord and a breakdown in their understanding of each other and of their relationship.

Having been initially happy to accept their differences, they had reached a point where each wanted the other to change: Sarah explicitly, wanting more time and intimacy with Jackie; and Jackie implicitly, wanting Sarah *not* to want these things. The breakthrough came when Jackie realised that she wanted Sarah to change just as much as Sarah wanted her to change, whereupon they both remembered again how much they had always appreciated one another. The breakthrough provided them with the opportunity to work towards compromise and in this way to once again find consensus, both sexually and in time spent together.

Story Seven

Tom and Adriana

We can't agree on trying for a baby

The Background

Tom and Adriana had just completed two unsuccessful rounds of IVF (In Vitro Fertilisation)—a technique to help people with fertility problems to have a baby—when they came to see me.

Both in their late thirties, they had been together for nine years and trying for a baby for six before they began IVF. Adriana felt 'a very strong longing for a child', and it was she who researched and organised the IVF. Tom wanted children, but said he 'didn't feel as strongly about it' as Adriana.

Although they might have been eligible for NHS treatment, they had decided they might have a shorter wait using a private clinic. The two rounds they had tried so far had used up most of their savings and at that point Tom wanted to stop. He felt that, as well as being expensive; the IVF was 'negatively affecting our relationship', leaving Adriana 'exhausted and miserable' and Tom 'fed-up and worried'.

Tom and Adriana had met by chance—both had used dating apps to look for a partner, but they met when they both reached for the same packet of soap powder in a corner supermarket. They recognised each other from a dating app, laughed, and got talking.

Both described their relationship as 'good'. He was a graphic designer, 'easy-going and not easily ruffled', while Adriana, an office manager, was the 'organised and prepared' one. 'We always fitted together well,' Tom said. 'Addy made sure the bills were paid on time and I made sure we had fun together.' Or, as Adriana put it, 'Tom is spontaneous, while I tend to plan. We're opposites, but mostly that works for us.'

Both Tom and Adriana were 'concerned and disappointed' when they didn't conceive naturally. Tom felt he could 'live with that' but for Adriana the idea of not having children was 'impossible'. They underwent medical tests which showed that there was nothing obvious to stop them conceiving naturally. After that they tried to conceive for another year by monitoring Adriana's ovulation, which meant, as Tom put it, 'having sex on prescription'.

When that did not work, Tom agreed to use their savings for the IVF. Both of them had been 'bitterly disappointed' when the first and then the second round failed. At that point, Tom wanted to stop, but Adriana was determined to continue.

Adriana explained that she was one of six children from a Romanian family, and she had always imagined that she would have several children of her own. Tom, on the other hand, was an only child and, while he had always imagined he would have a child, he felt he could live without children if need be.

The financial sacrifice involved meant that they hadn't had a holiday for a couple of years, and both felt that the IVF had come to dominate their lives.

An additional issue had also arisen. Tom had been told that to increase their chances of conceiving he should give up alcohol and take vitamin supplements, but he had not done either of those things and that had led to Adriana accusing him of 'sabotaging' her efforts.

It was Tom who suggested they come to see me, to help them to decide whether to have a third round of IVF, since they had reached an impasse.

My Initial Response
I felt a sense of pressure and I thought of a change of focus had occurred in what they both wanted from their relationship. I thought too of the strength of the feelings that Adriana was experiencing, driving an apparent urgency. Being male-bodied, I thought about how it was easier for me to understand how Tom might be feeling and I also thought about how it was Tom who wanted to come for therapy.

I suspected that their togethering was unable to make sense of Adriana's needs and that the gap in understanding had led to a polarising of positions, with Adriana putting greater emphasis on the IVF and Tom putting greater emphasis on other areas of life.

My thought was that the sudden arrival of the need for starting a family was something that neither had been able to understand, either individually or together, and how it was important for them both to feel heard by each other.

Certainly, the pressure to start a family had disturbed their energy together, and so had their level of consensus around how they should live in order to become pregnant.

In Session

'He only had two small things to do,' Adriana says bitterly. 'I had to go through all the horrible injections to stimulate egg production and then the whole invasive business of egg collection and then having the foetuses implanted. And what did he need to do? Just swallow a few vitamins and do without beer for a few weeks. And for all I know he ruined the whole thing for us.'

Tom looks weary. 'That isn't all I had to do, actually. I had to go with you to the clinic every time, give you the injections, look after you when you felt sick and bloated from the drugs, give semen samples and then go through the whole waiting process with you. And no, I didn't give up drinking and take the vitamins because I'd been told that my sperm count is fine and healthy, and it just felt like a step too far.'

'It seems to me that you are both voicing exasperation at the moment? My word, but is that right?' I say.

Tom nods, and Adriana shrugs and then mutters, 'that's an understatement.'

'Exasperation is an understatement—okay, is there a word that feels right for you?'

'Oppressed,' says Adriana. 'I want this so much and Tom doesn't.'

'So, Adriana, you feel that you want to go ahead with a third round of IVF, while Tom, you want to stop. Is that right?' I say.

'Yes,' Tom says, 'I just feel drained with it all. I'm afraid that we're losing what we have together. Adriana's always tired and down and I don't know how to get close to her anymore.'
Adriana looks at him and then back to me. Her expression is sad. 'Tom is right,' she says, 'I'm pretty miserable to be around these days. But I just can't give up on the idea of having a baby.

After all we've been through, I feel I deserve to have a child. I keep thinking that next time it must work out.'

'Even though with each round our chances go down,' Tom says. 'I honestly think we'd have a better chance if we just let all of this medical stuff go, and got back to being us.'

'You *would* think that, 'Adriana snaps. 'But if we don't plan and prepare it won't just magically happen.'

'I see that you're coming from very different places,' I say.

I hold both hands in front of me. 'On one hand of this continuum you've got planning and on the other you've got spontaneity,' I indicate one hand and then the other. 'You're in different positions here, so I wonder if I can invite each of you to move towards the other position.'

'Ha,' Adriana looks at Tom. 'I can't imagine living with the chaos in your wardrobe.'

'And I don't want to have to Google-calendar every moment of my day,' Tom shoots back.

Adriana starts to say something more, but then stops and sits back, as if she has suddenly deflated. Tom strokes his beard and looks out of the window.

'I am thinking about sadness,' I offer.

For a minute or so there is silence.

'I do feel for you, with all you've had to go through,' Tom says, turning to Adriana. 'You've been incredibly brave. I'm not sure I could have taken all the injections and side-effects and medical procedures you've had to put up with.'

Adriana nods. 'Thank you.' She pauses. 'I know I'm not much fun to be around at the moment. I guess I haven't been for a while. I can see you must feel as if you've lost a lot.'

Tom takes her hand. 'I love you. And I want a baby too. I just don't want to lose us.'

Adriana looks at him, tears in her eyes. 'I don't want to lose us either. You give me so much, you make me laugh, you remind me to lighten up and take time out, like that time you cheered me up with a trip to the sea. We had such a lovely day.' Tom smiles. 'And I need you to keep us organised. I'd be like a headless chicken without you.'

'You would,' Adriana says.

They both start laughing.

The Moment
The shift to understanding came for Tom and Adriana when I suggested that they each move closer to the position of the other—in other words, try to imagine what it might be like to be in the other one's shoes. What came through for both of them, initially, was a lot of sadness. This allowed them to pause and reflect and once they began to do that, both were able to appreciate what the other had been through. My offering of sadness appeared to soften their opposing stances, enabling them to reconnect with what they loved about one another.

What Happened Next
In the sessions that followed, Tom and Adriana agreed to take a six-month break from IVF before making a decision about whether they would try a third round. Tom had made the request and although for Adriana it was a difficult decision, in the end she agreed that it would give them time to recover from what they had been through in the previous couple of years and to have a holiday and spend time together.

They decided to take a month off from their jobs and to go as volunteers to help in a refugee camp on the Greek island of Lesbos, something they had talked about doing in the past and which meant a lot to both of them. Although they had to commit to several hours work a day, it also gave them a complete change of scene.

After the trip, both Tom and Adriana said that they had loved being away from their jobs and spending time together while doing something they both felt was important.

Two months later, they arrived in the therapy room smiling and announced that Adriana was pregnant—they had conceived naturally, and they both believed that stress had been a significant part of the problem.

At that point they left therapy, but the following year I received a warm card containing a photograph of Tom and Adriana with their baby, Nita.

My Reflections

Tom and Adriana's ways of being were very different: he spontaneous and she a planner. It had worked well for them in the past, but when they hit difficulties in having a family their attitudes began to diverge and tension set in. There was something around the sense of urgency felt by Adriana that was missed and so it was natural that Adriana and Tom would fall back on their differing ways of being rather than combining them to try to keep a balance.

Often, the arrival of the felt need for children for the female-bodied is so powerful and seemingly so instant that relationships struggle to make the time, space, and energy needed to integrate this natural phenomenon. Focus turns to management rather than acceptance; naturally so, given the pressure that it can put on other areas of life.

When it came to continuing with IVF, Tom and Adriana's togethering was affected by their difference in energy. Tom felt his energy for the project had run out, while Adriana was determined to continue. But when we began to look a little deeper it became clear that Adriana was also feeling tired and struggling with her energy levels.

When energy is low and one or both partners feel drained, it can affect all aspects of the relationship. Tom and Adriana's togethering was affected as they struggled to find consensus on whether to continue with IVF or not.

In such a situation the partners can find they are putting what little energy they have into arguing, rather than pausing and looking at ways to replenish and recover. The arguments go round and round and they both become increasingly weary, without accomplishing anything.

When Tom and Adriana were able to pause and see one another through fresh eyes, they realised that they both needed to take time out to recover their energy and their togethering. As they pursued a different course and stopped arguing about the IVF, both of them felt a release of tension, energetic recovery, and rediscovered consensus.

Story Eight

Patrick and Keisha

Since the accident I don't know if we still have a marriage

The Background

Patrick and Keisha met five years ago in her home country of South Africa. Patrick, a 'keen cyclist', had travelled with a good friend to take part in the famously gruelling eight-day Absa Cape race in the Western Cape. After the race, Patrick had stayed on for a week in Cape Town where he met Keisha, who was there visiting friends. They 'fell in love' and for the next two years they took it in turns to travel back and forth from Keisha's home in Johannesburg to Patrick's in London.

Keisha worked as a researcher for a pharmaceutical company and when Patrick asked her to marry him and move to the UK, her employers were happy to offer her a transfer to their British branch. Although it was 'hard' moving away from her parents and three siblings, Keisha was 'excited about marriage to Patrick and new opportunities in my working life'.

Patrick and Keisha settled halfway between her job in Reading and his as a civil engineer based in London, and both described their life together as 'full-on and demanding'. Both agreed they were 'determined and driven', with challenging jobs. In addition, Patrick continued his passion for long-haul cycling, training most evenings, and Keisha spent time at the gym after work as well as studying for an extra qualification. At weekends they often held dinners, cooking South African food for their friends.

Six months before they came to see me, Patrick had a cycling accident. He was 'knocked off his bike by a car' and his ankle was 'shattered'. He spent two weeks in hospital before being sent home with 'a walking stick and a physiotherapy plan'. Progress was 'slow' and as Patrick began to 'wonder whether he would ever cycle again,' he became 'withdrawn and depressed', spending his evenings 'watching television and losing interest in seeing friends and in spending time with Keisha'.

Worried about his downward spiral, Keisha said she 'encouraged' Patrick to 'see his cycling friends' and to get involved in other aspects of cycling, like route planning and product design. But Patrick felt Keisha was 'nagging' him and he reacted by becoming 'even more withdrawn'. As a child he had been sent to boarding school and he had learned 'to keep feelings hidden', so when Keisha asked him to talk about what was happening, he 'felt unable to'.

'He was depressed,' Keisha said. 'And depression scares me. I just watched him disappearing into a dark place.'

When Keisha's boss offered her a project to manage back in South Africa for six months she was tempted. It was a promotion, and it would mean she could spend time with her family. Would Patrick mind her going? She had 'begun to wonder if he would even notice—or care'. When she spoke to him about it, he told her that of course she must accept it. 'He didn't seem worried about me leaving,' Keisha said. 'I began to wonder if we still had a marriage.'

Keisha was at Heathrow airport, in the departure lounge, waiting for her flight, with her single glass of rosé champagne, when she had a memory of the two glasses she and Patrick had shared in that same lounge, waiting for a trip they had made to Thailand the previous year. It had been 'such a happy time' and she suddenly felt 'overwhelming sadness'. So Keisha did something she had never done before; she missed her flight and went home to tell Patrick that she had 'realised that I was starting to give up on our relationship but wanted to see if we could save it'. Patrick, 'stunned that she had not gone to South Africa', and even more stunned to hear what she was saying about their relationship, agreed to go to therapy to talk about what, in Keisha's words, 'we couldn't seem to talk about on our own'.

After two sessions, I got a message from Keisha that Patrick couldn't make the next one. I suggested that she come on her own and that we even things up by Patrick meeting with me individually for the following session. She checked with Patrick, and they told me they were happy to do that. When I asked her what it was like being in the therapy session without Patrick she said, 'I miss him.'

'Is that familiar?' I asked her.

'Yes, she replied. 'I feel I've lost him; the old Patrick would have been here, but nowadays he often drops out of things.'

'Have you ever told him you miss him?' I ask.

'Umm, no I don't think either of us has ever used that word with each other, although I say it all the time with my family in South Africa.'

The following week, I saw Patrick on his own. I asked him what had happened that meant he could not make the previous session.

'I wasn't feeling well.'

'Not feeling well?' I ask.

He shifted in his seat. 'I guess I should be honest. I just couldn't be bothered. I thought, what does it matter?'

'Can I ask what you think it was like for Keisha having the session without you?'

'I think she probably enjoyed having the chance to talk with you alone,' he replied, with little apparent emotion.

A week later I saw them together again.

My initial Response

The main feeling that I noticed in thinking about my initial interactions with Keisha and Patrick was desperation. I thought about Patrick's possible desperation about how to feel the same in life without his former level of fitness and I thought about Keisha's desperation that might come from not being able to convey how she missed him. I wondered what it was in the dynamic between them that had the power to silence her.

I was drawn to their engaging in terms of how Keisha's 'attempts to encourage' were experienced by Patrick as 'nagging'. I knew from both of them that neither wanted the relationship to end and so I wondered how their behaviour—Patrick's withdrawal and Keisha's tendency towards acceptance of that withdrawal—could somehow be interrupted.

Often, couples come to therapy when one of them is experiencing depression and so I know that typically the depressed partner withdraws, and the other partner does not know what to do. Both partners may try to tolerate what is happening in the hope that it will go away but the increasing distance and mounting unresolved hurt means that this is a flawed strategy.

In Session

'When I think about your relationship I think about how a distance has opened up between you,' I say.

'Not for me,' says Patrick.

'Yes,' Keisha says quietly.

Patrick is silent. Finally, he speaks. 'Keisha was going to abandon me, go back to South Africa for six months, which might as well be forever as far as I'm concerned.'

'You didn't even try to stop me,' Keisha says.

'What would be the point?' Patrick replies.

'Hmmm, *abandon*. I wonder which of you felt abandoned first?' I ask gently.

Keisha starts to cry. 'I can tell you when I first felt abandoned,' she says, turning to Patrick. 'Four weeks after the accident, on the Sunday when you wouldn't come and have brunch with me on the terrace.

'We always did that when the weather allowed,' she says, turning back to me. 'It was our thing, we loved it. That Sunday I sat on my own while Patrick stayed in bed and I missed him. I saw a squirrel stealing the bird food and I knew Patrick would have laughed at that; we'd have laughed together. But he wasn't there.'

'I missed you,' she says to Patrick, and she begins to cry.

I look at Patrick and I think he looks confused.

'What's it like to know that Keisha misses you?'

'I don't know,' he says, looking out of the window.

'Have you ever missed or been missed by anyone?' I ask.

'Well,' he says, and he thinks for a minute. 'I was sent to boarding school at seven and I missed my dog Kipper so badly. She was a Labrador, the same age as me; we had always been together. I missed Kipper more than I missed my parents, because they never seemed to notice whether I was there or not, but Kipper loved me. Every holiday I couldn't wait to get back to see her, but one day I came home and when I got to the garden gate, she wasn't in her usual spot waiting for me. I realised then that she was gone. She had died while I was at school and my parents hadn't even told me. I hated them from that moment on. I missed her so much and I couldn't bear to think about her dying without me there.'

Keisha is looking confounded by what she is hearing him say.

'I am sorry to hear that Patrick . . . that sounds so painful and such an important moment in your life.' I say.

'Yes,' he says, and he looks at Keisha. 'I don't ever allow myself to think about missing you or you missing me. I've been feeling so damned sorry for myself and I couldn't think straight. I thought I would just hold you back, now I can't do so many of the things we used to do.'

'I don't want to do those things without you,' Keisha says, wiping away her tears. 'You are what matters to me, not the things we do, or even work. I took that job because I felt you were pushing me away.'

Keisha reaches over to Patrick and hugs him. And he puts his arms round her and hugs her back.

The Moment

For Patrick and Keisha, the moment of comprehension and revelation came after I asked Patrick whether he had ever missed anyone. Until then they had struggled to recognise that they had not been talking about missing each other. But when he recalled the pain of the separation from his childhood dog, he began to understand Keisha's sense of loss. He also saw that, while he felt that she had abandoned him, his withdrawal from their life together and their struggle to speak about the impact of it on their relationship meant that it was in fact Keisha who had felt abandoned first.

What Happened Next

In the weeks that followed, Patrick and Keisha made the decision to move to South Africa so that Keisha could take up the six-month contract, which her boss had kindly agreed to defer for a couple of months.

Patrick became quite excited about the move. He decided to leave his job, which he felt had become very draining. He felt that the time in South Africa would allow him to re-evaluate what he wanted to do. It would also, crucially, allow him to work on healing his ankle; they planned to rent a house with a pool so that he would be able to swim daily to strengthen it.

A few months later I received an email from them telling me that they had decided to stay in South Africa. Keisha's work was going well, and she loved being near her family, while Patrick's ankle had healed and he was beginning to cycle again, although over much shorter distances. He had also decided to change career and had begun work as a youth coach, working with teenagers in a youth academy, teaching sports and life skills.

My Reflections

When a major life event, such as a serious accident, happens in the life of two partners, it can change everything, and this is what happened for Patrick and Keisha. They had first connected over their shared levels of ambition, energy, and drive. Together they led a high-octane, active lifestyle that they both loved. Patrick's accident and the depression he suffered as a result changed that, altering their togethering in every way. They spent their time together differently, their energy levels no longer matched, their verbal and non-verbal communication became disconnected, and they no longer found consensus on where they were in life and in their relationship.

The disconnect was revealed through their differing perceptions of what was happening in their engaging, specifically Keisha's view that she was 'encouraging' Patrick and Patrick's view that she was 'nagging'. This was a window through which their misunderstanding could be considered. Simply put, Patrick did not understand the impact of his withdrawal on Keisha, while Keisha did not understand the importance of that for Patrick.

It had all been a devastating blow for what had been a happy relationship. Neither Patrick nor Keisha knew how to navigate this new set of circumstances, and their reaction was to fear that the relationship could not withstand the pressure it was under.

Both chose to pull further apart—Keisha by going to South Africa and Patrick by withdrawing even further and refusing to show that he cared whether she left or not.

Keisha's decision not to take her flight, triggered by memories of happier times with Patrick, threw the relationship a lifeline and at that point they came to therapy. For me, seeing their sense of loss and grief at what had happened, it was important to enable them both to access their sadness. Neither Patrick nor Keisha was used to expressing painful emotions verbally, so when Keisha said she'd missed Patrick it was a significant step forward. For Patrick to meet her in this and let down the protective wall he had built around himself, he needed to access deeply buried feelings of loss, and he was able to do so by recalling the death of his dog.

Patrick and Keisha needed to find a new sense of togethering as they navigated the new reality of Patrick's injury and the impact it was having on their lives. Sometimes for this to happen, there needs to be a literal shift in life, whether it's moving home, moving jobs or moving locations. In the end they did all three, allowing Patrick to recover his sense of self and their relationship to find its new footing.

Story Nine

Zara and Scott

We've lost the connection between us

The Background

Zara and Scott are both actors. They met eight years ago, when they both appeared in the same theatre production. Both have been married before: Zara twice, and Scott once. She has two sons and he has a daughter, all of whom have left home.

In the production where they met, Zara had a 'leading role' and Scott was 'a more minor character'. When Zara asked for a day off to go to the funeral of a close friend, suggesting that her understudy might step in, the director flatly refused, and Zara became 'deeply upset'. Scott, finding her crying in her dressing room, suggested they 'go over her contract'. He found a clause that allowed for an absence of a day for personal reasons, which included funerals. As a result, the director allowed Zara the leave of absence. She was 'enormously grateful' to Scott for his support and offered, in return, to rehearse his scenes with him, which he 'appreciated' as he had been 'feeling uncertain about his character's motivation'.

A few weeks after meeting, on a walk along the Thames in London, they sat together on a bench looking at the Houses of Parliament and 'shared a moment' which they now laughingly speak about because, although they didn't realise it at the time, they had had 'exactly the same thought about each other: 'We were soulmates'.

Both acknowledge that their styles are very different—he is 'more practical', while she is a 'perfectionist and creative,' but they felt that they were 'a perfect balance for one another, able to provide mutual support'.

Within months of meeting they were living together in her flat in Wandsworth. Two years later, they married at Chelsea Town Hall.

Soon after their marriage, Scott was offered a major role in an ongoing year-round television drama and his contract has been renewed each year since then. Scott works 'long hours, often six days a week, with a tight schedule and scripts to learn overnight,' but his work has been 'well-paid' and so he and Zara have been able to buy a 'larger home in north London' closer to the TV studios where he works.

Zara's work continues to be 'stage-based' and recently she 'set up a theatre group'. She asked Scott to get involved with her group, and when he told her that he 'simply didn't have the time' a row ensued. Zara accused Scott of 'selling out' by taking television work in a soap opera, and he accused her of 'living in cloud cuckoo land' because her theatre work does not provide enough income for them to live on.

After that row and several others that ensued, they came to see me. In our initial session, both said that the other had 'changed'. Zara felt that Scott had become 'materialistic and arrogant' while Scott felt that Zara took his 'hard work and income for granted', enjoying the home and lifestyle his income afforded them while 'looking down on' his work.

In the next session, Scott said they had a holiday in Tuscany planned.

'We used to love travelling together,' he said. 'But these days Zara drives me mad. She's never packed until the morning we're travelling, and she thinks it's fine to get to the airport at the last second. It gets me so stressed; I like to be packed a day or two ahead and to leave plenty of time to relax at the airport.'

'He's a fusspot,' Zara replied. 'I hate packing, so I leave it until I have to do it. He used to think that was charming! Now he has to have everything planned and it takes all the joy out of it. He orders a car to the airport, but I used to love us doing it all on the hop, we'd laugh about running for the train to the airport.'

'Until you missed a train, and we missed our flight,' Scott said. 'I'm getting older. These days I just like to know everything is organised.'

'Might as well book the care home now,' Zara said crossly. 'We're not old, and I don't want to behave as if we are.'

'Have you changed your behaviours, or have you just run out of energy?' I ask, and they tell me it has always been like that.

'Okay, so it's something about energy,' I say. 'Tell me, do you both enjoy your work?'

'Yes' they both say, with energy and without hesitation.

Following that exchange, I suggested that for their upcoming trip they might like to try travelling to the airport separately, to see what it would be like for them to do something different.

They agreed to this and as they were booking their next session with me, Scott said, 'I don't suppose you would consider coming to see us at our home, would you? I've got to be back on set the next day and it would be a real help.'

I told them that I would be happy to come to their home.

Two weeks later, after they had returned from their trip, I go to see them at their house, close to Hampstead Heath in north London. Scott opens the door and shows me around a large, bright, basement kitchen, an open-plan living room looking out onto a mature garden, and several bedrooms. The impression is of a glamorous and tasteful home, furnished in minimalist style, much of it white and cream. I notice that Zara does not come with us on the tour of the house.

We settle in the living room, where there are two large, cream sofas and several armchairs.

My Initial Response

I was mostly greatly impacted hearing about the moment they shared about both thinking they were soulmates. I thought about it as a moment of communion and about the context in which it had occurred, after they had been able to navigate a problem together. I suspected that this gave them faith in the potential for them to spend time together. Zara sharing her feelings at not being able to go to the funeral and Scott's full understanding acceptance of how she felt enabled them to find a solution together. Zara's ability to express her feelings and Scott's ability to think about a possible practical solution captured their differing ways of being.

I noticed that I had feelings that make sense through the words *heavy* and *turgid*, and it led me to think about how they both seemed to have retreated into their own ways of being.

I also thought about their having lost trust in their ability to work together when either of them was unhappy. An image of a boxing ring came to mind, which placed me in the role of referee. My most natural style of thinking about life tends towards the analytical—looking for patterns, connections, and meanings, and yet with them I felt a need to be more practical and more interventionist, which felt both exciting and risky.

Setting a practical task was one element, but then I wondered about my agreeing to and being excited about the home visit and whether my doing so was 'really in the service of the therapy.' I thought about how the home visit would provide me with a great deal of information and I made a mental note to explore with them what my agreeing to the home visit might mean for them.

In Session

'I'm wondering how it is for you both that I am here?'

'It's nice to be able to show you where we live,' says Scott.

Zara is silent.

I notice a photograph of a pretty cottage on the table next to the armchair where she is sitting, and Zara catches my glance.

'That's our cottage in Stratford-upon-Avon,' she says. 'I love it there; I try to go as often as I can. It's very small compared to this place, but I feel so free and at ease when I'm there.'

'Are you there often?' I ask.

'She's there more than here,' Scott answers. 'I can't get away that often, so Zara goes, but it means we spend less time together. Sometimes I think she prefers it to this house.'

'I like this house,' Zara says. 'But I never really feel comfortable here. There's always so much to manage—cleaners, gardeners, decorators—I love the cottage because there's none of that, it's just easy. I can spend the afternoon painting and not notice time passing. Here, I never get time to paint.'

'At least you get to spend time here,' Scott says. 'I get home from work, learn my lines, sleep, and go back to work—so that I can keep paying for the house I barely see.'

Zara frowns at him. 'I never asked you to pay for it,' she mutters. 'I would be perfectly happy in the cottage.'

'Where I can't be, because I need to be based here for work,' Scott says, sighing.

Tell me about your trip,' I say. 'Did you travel to the airport separately? How was that for each of you?'

Zara turns to me, and she smiles. 'We did. And I really enjoyed it. I got the train and I enjoyed looking out of the window, reading my magazine, and having a coffee.'

How was it for you?' I ask Scott.

'It was all right,' he says. 'I booked a car, as usual, I slept on the way—as usual—and I got there early and had a drink until it was time to meet Zara.'

'And what was it like for you both when you met at the airport?' I ask.

'I felt relieved,' says Scott. 'Strangely, me too,' says Zara.

'Strangely?' I ask. 'Well, I thought that Scott would not be so happy to see me,' she laughs.

Scott looks at her. 'Me too,' he says.

'How come?' I ask.

'Well, I thought that now he had everything his own way he wouldn't want me anymore,' Zara says.

'I thought the same,' Scott nods.

'So you both do things differently, but when you do things in your own way you fear something?' I say.

They look at me as though the question makes sense but neither speaks. They seem stuck.

'I wonder if what you fear in those moments is rejection?' I venture.

Scott suddenly straightens up, losing his deflated posture, while Zara's posture relaxes. They look at each other and I sense that something is understood between them as they smile and there is a sense of ease.

The Moment

For Zara and Scott, the moment of understanding came when I asked them about their experience of being back together after both agreeing to do something differently and separately. In that moment of connection they realised that though they are very different in many ways, it was not, ultimately, a reason why either of them would not want the other.

What Happened Next

During the following sessions, Zara and Scott talked about their London house and came to recognise that they both, in their own ways, felt oppressed by it. They took the decision to sell the house and buy somewhere smaller, reducing the cost and the time spent managing the house.

Zara had begun to feel that Scott did not need her in the way that he used to and Scott was fearing that Zara preferred being in the cottage on her own to being with him, but as they explored those fears they both came to see that it they were only able to do what they were doing because of the lives they had co-created and they were reminded of all that they used to do together and enjoy. Ultimately, they each wanted the other to be happy, and having understood that they were both actually deeply happy in their work, change was possible.

In this way, they began to offer one another the mutual support that they were both missing. In practice, this meant that they did spend less time together as they split their time between the London and country homes, with Scott spending more of the time in London and Zara in the country home. They were at ease with that because they both had renewed energy, which enabled them to do the work they loved. At the same time, they were very protective of and put great emphasis on the time that they were able to spend together, which left them feeling secure, happy, supported, connected, and relaxed.

My Reflections

Zara and Scott were initially united by their desire to meet a soulmate. This connection at first masked their very different ways of being. They enjoyed a degree of mutual dependency, but at the same time their felt sense of security came from being able to express their creativity. For Scott, his self-expression focused on his impact on others as an actor, while for Zara it was more about how she felt in herself.

Their togethering was disrupted by the demands of Scott's new television role, which meant that they could not spend the time together that they'd once had. For Scott, life became one of constant pressure; the demand to work long hours and to fit everything around that. Although he was compensated financially, enabling them to buy a glamorous home, they found that neither of them fully enjoyed it. A sense of unease had crept in, and they were both holding onto a lifestyle with which neither felt fully comfortable. What was not understood between them was that they didn't need to do everything together, or in the same way, to be happy. They had forgotten that their differing ways of being and their individual sense of ease in those differing ways was not a threat but an asset to their relationship.

To begin to shift the situation they needed to be reminded of how things used to be before they met, and their separate journeys to the airport provided the first step in that realisation. In being allowed to be themselves, and then realising that they wanted each other despite their differing ways, their faith in the relationship was restored, and with that came a sense of ease that also energised them, enabling them to work together to ensure they managed life in a way that supported what made them both happy.

Story Ten

Marcus and Tian

He avoids talking to me about how he feels

The Background

Marcus and Tian had been together for eighteen months when they came to see me. In their email they said that as gender and sexually diverse partners, they needed to speak about how to open up their relationship.

During their first session they told me that they had met at a gay male sauna. Both had gone there for sex: neither had expected to begin a relationship there. 'We got talking after we had sex and I told Tian it was great to be with such a sexy man,' Marcus said. 'And I told him that I actually identify as non-binary,' Tian added.

'I was surprised and intrigued,' Marcus said. 'I wanted to know more. I really liked talking to them—it felt easy and so I asked for Tian's number, and I called the next day. We met up and we got on well. Tian was a lot of fun and very easy to be with. I did struggle a bit with the pronouns,' he said, pulling a face. 'But I love that Tian is non-binary—it's something that seems so free and personal, nothing to do with what anyone else thinks or wants.'

'While you were Mr Uptight, weren't you, Spudge?' Tian said, laughing.

'Spudge?' I asked.

'Tian's nick name for me,' Marcus laughed. 'We weren't an obvious match,' he agreed. 'Tian is from Harehills in Leeds and I'm from commuter-belt Surrey.'

'Where I grew up you wouldn't go out alone at night,' Tian added. 'I went to a school where the career of choice for most kids was drug-dealing.'

'And I went to a ridiculously expensive boarding school,' Marcus said. 'But it was actually awful, I hated it. I was lonely and miserable and my nickname there was Pansy.'

Tian, who worked with young offenders on reparation schemes, moved into Marcus's London flat a few months after they met. Marcus was a banker, working long hours, and his flat was, as Tian put it, 'like a perfect but completely impersonal hotel suite. I felt *so* not at home'.

'When Tian first arrived they looked upset. I assumed it was just about the change but then a few nights in I heard them crying. They had left the bed and was on their own in the living room. Tian told me they were unhappy and I was so confused.' 'Yes, completely useless,' laughed Tian, 'Spudge had no idea that I felt out of place. It didn't feel like home to me and I didn't feel able to change it in any way.'

'As soon as I understood I told Tian that I longed for them to feel at home and that I was happy for them to change things around. And crikey, Tian made such a difference to the place. I felt a bit uncomfortable having loads of new things around but now I find it really nice.'

'I softened all those hard edges,' Tian said, 'so that we could actually relax there and feel it was a home, not just a place to sleep.'

The two of them had recently been on a holiday together and Marcus had invited a third person to join them for sex one night. Tian had not objected in principle but had felt uncomfortable about the way it happened.

'We had talked about opening up the relationship, bringing in other people,' Tian said. 'I said I wanted some agreement between us about the way we would do that. Would it always be someone joining both of us, or would we see other people separately? I thought we should decide how we wanted it to work before we went ahead. But every time I tried to talk to Marcus about how we both felt, he would grab an energy drink and then change the subject.

'Then we go on holiday and Marcus arrives in our room with someone in tow and I'm just expected to go along with it. To be honest I felt hacked off because it should have been something we did together. I didn't really feel part of it and while we did start off having sex, the three of us, I felt left out. In the end I said, "I'll leave you two to it," and then I went down to the beach and cried. When I went back to the room I tried to talk to

Marcus about it, but he just got angry and said I shouldn't have left.'

My initial Response

The word *violent* came to my mind when I reflected on the strength of the alienation between Tian and Marcus: both when they moved in together and then the night of the attempted threesome. The word *consent* seemed relevant, and I thought of the power of feelings at times when things take place that have not been explicitly and fully consented to by the partners.

Tian and Marcus's *engaging*, in terms of the depth of understanding it facilitated, impacted their ability to agree. Both home and sex are such deeply personal areas for us individually that understanding and agreeing in those areas is a challenge for all partnerships.

Returning to the word *violent*, I thought about Marcus's history in relation to bullying, because when there has been bullying, the parties involved have experience of behaviours without consent, and the hurt and trauma caused often becomes apparent in a disturbance in how consent is not navigated. In thinking about Tian, I wondered what was happening so that instead of stating an opinion and a request, there was instead a withdrawal.

In Session

'You said everything is fluid and open,' Marcus says angrily. 'That's your thing. And you agreed we could bring in other people.'

He reaches into his bag and brings out a can of energy drink. As he pulls the tab open, he looks at me and says, 'Do you mind if I drink this?'

'Well, it's okay for you to drink that,' I say. 'But at the same time, it needs to be okay if we have a conversation about why you want to drink it.'

Marcus looks confused. He is about to take a sip and then he hesitates. He puts the drink down and shrugs, before slumping back into the corner of the sofa where he and Tian are both sitting.

'What's happening?' Tian asks.

'I'm feeling flattened,' Marcus says.

Tian looks astonished. 'You just said how you feel. You never say how you feel.'

Marcus looks over at Tian and shrugs again.

'What was it that led to you feeling flattened?' Tian says.

After a pause, Marcus says, 'You kept wanting to talk but it didn't feel like a conversation to me. I didn't feel I had anywhere to go with it, there wasn't anything I could say that was right.'

Tian frowns, and then says, 'I remember a few months ago you got drunk, and you said I flattened you and I was a bully, and I was hurt, I didn't understand why. And then the next day when I asked you about it you couldn't remember. But I think I get it now.

'This is really hard for you, isn't it? Feeling bullied? It takes you back to when you were at school, doesn't it?'

There are tears in Marcus's eyes. Tian reaches a hand over and takes Marcus's hand and for a few moments both are silent.

The Moment

An example of consent in action between Marcus and me led to the moment of understanding. I asked Marcus to talk about why he wanted a caffeine-heavy drink during our session and Marcus, more used to relationships in which behaviour is either allowed or not allowed, expressed himself differently when he encountered my curiosity. His response was to deflate and Tian, filled with empathy, recognised that without the drink Marcus felt exposed and defenceless. It was the opening that allowed them a moment of deep connection and mutual recognition.

What Happened Next

Marcus and Tian went on to talk about the pattern they had established, in which Tian would remove himself when he felt really upset and would then try to talk to Marcus about it afterwards. Meanwhile Marcus, feeling confused and 'flattened' by Tian's criticism, would take action unilaterally in order to cope. In therapy this was revealed through his particular habit of reaching for an energy drink. In the past, when this happened, Tian would become frustrated and cross, but would nevertheless push on with attempting the conversation, while for Marcus the drink was an attempt to break the tension, change his feeling of low energy, and hope that his action would make the conversation stop.

Together, they worked out that Marcus's compulsion to take unilateral action was a way of coping with his discomfort when he felt confronted or under pressure, and this went back to his time at school when he experienced bullying and intimidation by older boys. The drink provided a crutch and a barrier for him, a way to keep himself safe.

Tian realised that in communicating with Marcus it was helpful to pay attention to the whole communication, including Marcus's body language, rather than just the spoken word and that saying to Marcus, 'are you comfortable with this? We don't need to go on if you're not comfortable,' would help.

In subsequent conversations the two of them revisited the awkward holiday experience and Marcus told Tian that in bringing a third person in on their holiday, he had thought he was doing something Tian would like. He had an image of what it was to be a man, based on his early experience in his family and at school, and this included making decisions on his own and 'pushing ahead,' with things, rather than choosing discussion and agreement.

Tian was surprised to hear Marcus say that he had always been in awe of how Tian seemed to be able to stand up to others and do what he wanted. Because of that it had shocked him that Tian had not felt able to be more direct about his unhappiness when Marcus brought a third person back to their room.

'I thought you would tell me if you were unhappy,' Marcus said. 'Your happiness comes first and if you say you want or do not want something then I want to know—I really cannot read your mind.'

Tian explained that it had actually led to feelings of exclusion and so the impulse had been to step back and let things happen, rather than to intervene by stepping forward and saying 'can we have a quick conversation about this'. Tian had thought Marcus was being selfish, while Marcus had intended the opposite—he had wanted it to be a good experience for both of them but especially for Tian.

Marcus admitted he had been very nervous, and Tian said, 'Actually, I did think you were nervous about it, but you were behaving as if you weren't and that was part of why I felt excluded'.

My Reflections

Marcus and Tian connected through a shared belief around choice and freedom. But although they had agreed they would like to have an open relationship, and they had consensus about it in theory, in practice and in the 'ing' of *engaging* and *agreeing*, there was misunderstanding. So often partners focus on rules and agreements about particular situations rather than the process by which they will together navigate new situations in the moments they arise. Of course, it is unrealistic *not* to plan or have agreements. However, partners need to feel able to navigate consensus at times when something previously agreed no longer feels right because if something isn't right for a partner then it won't be right for the relationship.

Often, partners try to get each other to stick to agreements rather than sticking to a process of engaging that will enable their agreeing to adapt as change comes along.

Tian and Marcus's pattern of engaging without a focus on consent meant that they were not able to engage and agree in highly emotive situations. Neither of them expressed their real feelings verbally, and with that level of disconnect between them, their mutual understanding broke down, so that neither of them knew what the other really wanted or felt. Marcus concealed his fears through action and also projecting a confidence and energy that was unlikely to be challenged, as he did by reaching for high-energy drinks.

In thinking about the use of any substance it can be helpful to be curious about what it is needed for. Exploration often reveals that someone is trying to cope but has not found any other way of doing so. This is often the way that compulsion, or addiction, works. The substance, whether it is high-energy drinks, drugs, alcohol, cigarettes, food or anything else, provides the person with a way of managing painful feelings.

So, rather than focusing on the substance, I will invite the person using the substance to talk about why they are choosing to use it.

When Marcus deflated, as he put the drink aside, it provided an opportunity for Tian to see Marcus with his defences down. And from that opening, the two of them were able to find a deeper communication, both verbally and non-verbally, redressing the imbalance in their togethering.

Ultimately, as with many partnerships, the stated reason for therapy turns out not to be what the therapy is really needed for. In this case, they didn't need therapy to discuss opening the relationship, but rather for deepening understanding and learning how to improve their engaging and agreeing.

Story Eleven

Flo and Bel

Our rows have become violent

The Background
Flo and Bel met fourteen years ago, when they were taking part
in the Duke of Edinburgh's Gold Award scheme. They had both
chosen climbing as their physical activity and they met while
attending weekly training sessions at the local climbing centre.

Flo was eighteen and Bel nineteen when they met. 'We had
noticed each other but we hadn't spoken. I guess we were both
a bit shy,' Bel said. 'Then one evening another climber, a
young boy, had a panic attack while he was at the top of the
climbing wall. He was safe, he had a rope on, but he just froze.
Flo was great, she talked him down, telling him where to put
each foot and hand.'

'It wouldn't have worked without Bel,' Flo said. 'She
calmed him down and reassured him; she reminded him that he
knew what to do and could get himself down.'

Afterwards they had gone for a coffee. 'We hit it off. We
had a lot in common,' Bel said. 'We were very fit, we loved
climbing, and we were both determined to become really good
climbers.'

By the time the climbing training ended they had become a
couple. But while climbing had bonded them and shown them
that they could work together in a challenging situation, they
discovered later that they were not as similar as they had first
thought. 'Flo is the practical one,' Bel said. 'I'm more of a
people person.'

In the years that followed, Flo went to university to study
law, and then she joined a law firm and eventually became a
fully-qualified solicitor. Bel 'didn't want to go to university,' so
she went to work for a well-known supermarket brand and
worked her way up to become a customer services manager, in
charge of a team. 'I love it,' she said. 'I spend my days sorting
out people's problems, which is what I do best.'

After Flo left university, she and Bel moved in together, round the corner from her mum, Annie. Flo was 'incredibly close' to her mum, and Bel 'soon got to love her too'. Annie had multiple sclerosis, so Flo and Bel would go round to see her most days, to help with shopping and chores. At least once a week they would stay for supper with Annie, who adored both of them.

A year ago Annie died, very suddenly. Both Flo and Bel were 'devastated' by her loss. 'We started arguing more,' Flo said. 'Well, we always argued, to be honest, but it never got out of hand. Annie used to sort us out.

'Now she's not there we seem to be fighting all the time. And last week we had a massive row. We pushed each other. That upset us, but a week later we ended up yelling at each other and then . . . smacking each other.'

That had prompted them to come to see me.

'In the video on your website you reminded us a bit of Annie,' Flo said. 'You had the same way of talking, in a calm and friendly way.'

The row that led to Flo smacking Bel, and Bel smacking Flo back had, they said, been about Bel's struggle with grief over losing Annie. 'We both missed her dreadfully,' Flo said. 'In some ways it felt like she was the glue holding us together. We spent so much time with her, and she could always see if one of us was upset or if we'd had an argument. She gave such simple, easy advice, but it worked. She made us see the best in each other, and she made us laugh.

'After she died we both felt lost, but I threw myself into work and it helped. But Bel just moped about feeling sorry for herself and it drove me mad.'

'I wasn't moping,' Bel said, 'I was grieving, and I needed time to just think and be on my own. Flo kept giving me advice, wanting me to go on a run with her or join a cookery class. When she told me to pull myself together I just lost it, I screamed at her and she whacked me over the face, so I whacked her back. It shocked us both, and we realised we had to do something and that's when we came to you.'

My Initial Response

I had the thought that while Flo and Bel might have been looking after Annie, Annie was actually looking after Flo and Bel's relationship and I wondered about the need for them to have someone around who spoke in a calm and friendly way and, beyond that, what calm and friendly actually was for them.

I registered their differing ways of approaching life: Flo as very action-oriented and Bel as reflective, and I suspected that these ways of being were somehow tempered through their love and care for Annie, in the same way that they worked together on the climbing wall.

I thought about the tension in relationships, about time together, and the balance between the various aspects of time together, energy, engaging and agreeing, and I suspected that in some way time with Annie validated both of them equally. It occurred to me that while struggling to grieve individually, their togethering may have been lost.

In Session

'I just can't bear Bel moping around all the time,' Flo says. 'Honestly, Annie was my mum, I should be the one taking it hardest. I miss her like crazy, but I don't mope, I get on and do my job and live my life because that's what she would have wanted. Sometimes I think Bel is just a bit of a drama queen.'

'How dare you call me that!' Bel snaps. 'It's nothing to do with what she would have wanted; it's just the way you are. You're always busy, always doing something, always pushing on. You're obsessive. That's not me; it's not what I do. I need time to just . . . be.'

'How are you going to move on by just "being"? That's ridiculous,' Flo says. 'There are plenty of things you could do to help yourself, but you won't. You're wallowing.'

'It's always your way is the only right way,' Bel says. 'You're so bossy. Why can't I be different to you and do it my way?'

Flo snorts and leans forward, her cheeks reddening and her voice raised. 'What are you talking about? You're so up yourself these days, I'm the one holding everything together. You barely even notice what needs doing in the house.'

I look from Flo to Bel. 'Are these sessions helpful?' I ask.

They both stop and look at me.

'Well, you're not helpful in the way Annie was,' Bel says. 'She used to really help.'

'Ah,' I say, 'so not helpful then?' I pause for a moment. 'I don't know whether this might be useful, but I am noticing that I have a lot of tension in my neck and shoulders.'

Flo stares at me. 'That's what Bel always says. She ends up really tense when we argue.'

'I do,' Bel says. 'Just the same as you described, it's all in my neck and shoulders.'

'I don't want to make you feel tense,' Flo says, looking at Bel. 'I argue for a living. I guess sometimes, well, maybe I don't know when to stop. I'm sorry.'

Bel's face changes. 'I know you don't want to make me feel tense. And I don't want to wind you up, either. I'm sorry too.'

They look at one another, anger gone, and softness in its place.

The Moment

When I shared my physical reaction to their argument, both Flo and Bel became aware of the impact their arguments have on another person—me—and more importantly, on each other. Flo realised that she was behaving as if she were at work and Bel realised she was putting up with something—the discomfort of physical tension—because she felt she should. Until that point, she had been unaware that her sense of tension had meaning. Both became aware, in that moment of understanding, that they were co-creating the situation.

What Happened Next

Flo and Bel had both realised that in their pattern of arguments, without the calming intervention of Flo's mother Annie, they were going to a place beyond useful; a place that was 'too hot', as Flo put it.

In the following sessions, they looked at ways to halt their arguments before they reached the point where things could escalate into tension or violence.

I suggested they use a signal, which they could agree would mean an immediate end to an argument.

'Do you remember we used to do that?' Bel laughed. 'When we were younger, we used to say putting two fingers in the air meant stop. I can't remember when we stopped doing that.'

'I can't either,' said Bel. 'Maybe we could use a word this time?'

'A gesture tends to be simpler, in the heat of the moment,' I said. 'Perhaps this time choose something more neutral than two fingers? Something easy to remember and non-aggressive?'

'How about this?' Bel said, putting her hands on her hips. 'It's clear, but it's not aggressive.'

Flo laughed, 'I like that. All right, we'll do that.'

As with anything new, it took some practice, but both Flo and Bel agreed that it worked. If one of them put her hands on her hips, then the argument had to end. They found the best way to do this was for one of them to leave the room for a few minutes.

'We've got pretty good at it,' Flo said, a few sessions later. 'We both respect it, and we stop, immediately. Bel tends to reach that point before I do, so she's usually the one with her hands on her hips first. I call it her 'huffy madam' look. But it brings me up short, I realise I'm going into 'work' mode again and I walk away, take some deep breaths and then go back and we start again on a different subject, or even with a joke.'

My Reflections

When arguments escalate into physical violence, it's important to stop before it becomes a pattern. Flo and Bel both understood this. Their relationship had always included plenty of rows and they were fine with that—they felt it was a part of who they both were—but they were shocked when a row escalated to the point where they slapped one another and this prompted their decision to come to therapy. I knew, therefore, that they were both committed to doing things differently and de-escalating their conflicts.

Their problem was that when Annie was alive she had been their means of de-escalation. Their mutual commitment to her and love for her, and hers for them, meant that their rows were defused early on. Without Annie to calm things, and with both of them feeling deep grief, they felt deprived of the means to prevent row from becoming violent.

I would not always choose to mention the impact people's behaviour in the therapy room might be having on me. But in this case I felt it might be useful. Sometimes, two people are so engrossed in the interaction between them that they are not aware of the impact they are having on anyone else present or on each other. My intervention caused them to pause, and to recognise the dynamic that was being created and its impact, emotionally and physically.

Flo and Bel did not have agreement or consensus about certain aspects of their lives–for instance the 'right' way to grieve for Annie—and that meant that they were unable to fully understand, appreciate, and support one another.

In situations like that I will often ask couples to agree on a very simple means of interrupting conflict; a sign that they both accept means 'stop'. With such an agreement they can regain consensus and avoid escalating conflict.

For Flo and Bel, who had used a sign in the past, this was valuable. They were not going to stop having rows—neither of them expected or even wanted this—but they did need to stop their rows before they became damaging. The use of a mutually agreed sign was also a symbol of support, because neither of them wanted to hurt or harm the other or be a person who would do so.

Story Twelve

Jasmin and Solomon

We can't find a way to agree, so is it time to split up?

The Background
Jasmin and Solomon are both in their early forties. They met
six years ago at an anthropology conference in London:
Jasmin's anthropology speciality is biological and Solomon's is
cultural. They bonded over their shared interest in, and
knowledge of, human behaviour.

At that time, Solomon was a widowed single parent with a
daughter, Maia, aged three, and Jasmin had recently left a long-
term relationship. After getting together they decided 'within
months' to move in together and get married. Jasmin moved
into Solomon's home and they married a year after meeting.
Both wanted another child and a year later Jasmin became
pregnant. Their son, Zac, is now three-and-a-half years old.
Solomon's daughter Maia is now nine.

They chose to do their therapy online and in their first
session, from separate screens in separate rooms, they told me
that they both felt their relationship was 'in trouble'.

'We have quite different parenting beliefs and styles,'
Jasmin said. 'This has really come to a head over our parenting
of Zac. At three he's full of energy and wanting to explore
everything and to constantly test us. I believe we should be firm
with him, with very set routines and rules, but for Solly the
opposite is true.'

'It's not that I don't believe in routines and rules,' Solomon
said. 'But for me it's about the child as a person. I want to
engage with him, find out who he is and what he wants and
relate to him. So, for instance, if he doesn't like a certain food, I
won't make him eat it, I'll prepare something else for him—I
don't eat foods I don't like, so why should he? But Jasmin
thinks he should eat what we give him, because it's nourishing
and balanced, and that letting him leave food or ask for
something else is indulging him.'

'It is,' Jasmin interjected. 'And if he eats a plate of rice and no vegetables it's unhealthy too. I don't think we should run rings around a small boy who doesn't know what's good for him.'

I asked whether they had disagreed over parenting Maia before Zac came along.

'Not so much,' Solomon said, 'because Jasmin was new in Maia's life, and Maia and I had our routines. Jasmin was very respectful about that, even though she didn't always agree with my way of doing things.'

'Remember when Maia developed asthma?' Jasmin said. 'That did show up our differences.'

'It did,' Solomon said. 'Jasmin wanted the route of doctors and medical tests and I was more concerned with what was happening in Maia's life. I worried that the loss of her mother might have triggered it. In the end we took both routes, we did check things out medically and I took her to a child therapist too.'

I pointed out that this seemed to be a good example of bringing their different approaches—Jasmin's more science-based biological interest and Solomon's more societal and cultural one—together.

'It was,' Jasmin agreed. 'And there are other times when we did manage to compromise, but with parenting Zac we just can't. Take bedtime, for instance. I think Zac should be in bed by quarter to seven, have a story read to him and lights out at seven. That way he gets adequate rest and we get a little time with Maia before her bedtime at seven-thirty, and then Solly and I can have the evening together. But Solly will spend hours getting Zac to sleep, reading to him, singing to him, lying on the bed with him. He did that with Maia but he's twice as bad with Zac. And Maia won't go to bed until Zac is settled, so we end up with the whole evening disrupted.'

'I don't see it that way,' Solomon replied. 'To me the child feeling safe, loved, and peaceful is paramount, and if that means I need to be there with him, then I want to be there. I always took that view with Maia and she doesn't need that kind of attention now. She outgrew it and she's quite independent at bedtime.'

Jasmin rolled her eyes at this. 'Studies show that if children have a fixed bedtime they will feel safer for it,' she said.

I asked whether they had tried their two separate styles, to see which was more effective.

'We did,' Jasmin said. 'I had two weeks of putting Zac to bed at seven and it was beginning to work, he was getting used to it, when Solomon disrupted the whole thing.'

'I couldn't bear how much he cried,' Solomon said. 'It wasn't working at all.'

'I don't agree,' Jasmin said.

Recently, a new issue had arisen. Zac's nursery teacher had told Jasmin and Solomon that Zac had begun showing concerning behaviour, with instances of aggression with the other children and increased distress, bursting into tears when gently reprimanded by the teachers.

Solomon and Jasmin were both 'deeply concerned' about this, and whether they were 'in some way responsible'. I asked them in what way they felt they might be responsible for Zac's change of behaviour.

When I see couples I will often meet both partners individually if they wish for it or agree to do so, and when, subsequently, I saw Solomon and Jasmin separately, I was struck by how much they had to say about one another that they had not said to each other. Each blamed the other's parenting for Zac's difficulties and when I asked about why they had not said those things to each other they both told me that they were nervous it would cause conflict.

In those separate sessions I got more of a sense of their individual ways of being and the context of their experience of relationships. In particular, they spoke to me about their individual beliefs around nature and nurture and how it connected to their own experiences. Solomon has in the past had feedback from others that led him to wonder about dyslexia, while Jasmin had feedback that made her think about whether she might have OCD (Obsessive Compulsive Disorder).

In the next session I saw them both together.

My Initial Response

Their shared curiosity around being human moved me and I asked myself whether I was confusing my own interest in the my thinking was being clouded by my own interests in the existential and therefore whether this was helpful? I wondered whether our interests, as a shared value, provided a foundation for them that led to communion and ease for them both. Clearly, with Zac's arrival, their togethering became in some way intolerable, and I had the sense that it was only just tolerable beforehand. I wondered whether they talked about that when they decided to have a child together.

I also found myself feeling defensive and under pressure to provide answers. They presented a disagreement on parenting, and yet I suspected that it was their individual sense of identity that felt under threat. I thought about just how much Jasmin and Solomon's beliefs and values were both embodied through the way in which they thought things should be done and their choice of careers, acting to further sediment their beliefs.

In Session

'I wonder if you are talking to one another about what you feel is causing Zac's change of behaviour at nursery?' I say.

Jasmin looks away from the screen for a moment. 'Not really,' she says. 'I guess I've tip-toed around what I really think. I haven't wanted to hurt Solomon, but I do think his parenting is causing the problem.'

'My parenting?' Solomon says. 'It's your parenting that's the problem, you're just too hard on him.'

'That's ridiculous,' Jasmin says. 'We're just not on the same page as parents, and we should be and that's making him feel insecure. Solomon is teaching him terrible habits, giving him too many choices that he's not ready for.'

'I'm just loving him and listening to who he is,' Solomon replies. 'What can be terrible about that?'

'It seems that you both have strongly held beliefs on nature and nurture,' I say. 'And it is hard for you to find a position that feels comfortable for you both?'

'That's right,' Jasmin says.

'So, when Zac does not go to bed at seven, as you would like, how does that make you feel?'

Jasmin thinks for a moment. 'Anxious,' she replies slowly. 'I feel so anxious, it makes me very stressed.'

'And Solomon, how do you feel when Jasmin insists that Zac go to bed on time, even if he says he's not tired?'

Solomon looks sad. 'I feel anxious too, if I'm honest,' he says.

The Moment

'It seems that what you are sharing here is a high level of anxiety?' I say.

They both nod.

'And this is perhaps what you have not said to each other? That the other person's parenting style gives you an elevated level of anxiety?

Again, they both say, 'Yes'.

At this point, they look at each other and pause.

'I've been thinking about the concerns you've both expressed, that you are having an impact in some way on Zac, and how when we've talked about it you weren't certain about what that might be,' I say. 'So I'm wondering whether Zac might be picking up your shared experience of anxiety?'

'The teacher did say something about anxiety,' Solomon says.

Jasmin looks thoughtful. 'Actually, now I think about it, in the past when Zac has been anxious he has shown some of the behaviours the teacher talked about.'

What Happened Next

I was alerted to a major shift when, in their next session two weeks later, Jasmin and Solomon joined the meeting on the same connection. They were, for the first time, sitting in the same room on the same sofa.

They talked about how they had agreed that they could not live with their different styles of parenting. Although they had connected over their shared love of, and interest in, humanity, they had very different views and beliefs, which they felt were integral to who they were, both in their work and in their lives outside work. Neither of them wanted to change and they did not feel that compromise was possible. The result of this openness with one another was the joint decision to split up. While it gave them a lot of sadness, they said, it also brought relief; both felt it was the right decision, for them and for the children.

Over the weeks that followed they continued to come to therapy so that they could 'agree the best possible way to part', as Solomon put it. That meant discussing where to live and how to share childcare. Agreement took time, but eventually they decided to sell their home and to buy new homes close to one another and to the children's schools, so that it would be easy for the children to go between the two. They also agreed to share parenting on an equal basis, with the children having their own rooms in each home.

Solomon and Jasmin told the children together of their decision and they took time to prepare the children for the changes that were to come.

Within a few weeks they said the teacher had reported that Zac's behaviour at nursery had become more settled.

'We know that we will be parenting him fairly differently, although we'll try to emphasise consistencies,' Jasmin said. 'But we also know that with two happy parents in two homes he can understand that Mum does it this way and Dad does it that way. It's been hard for us to accept that we are better apart, but all four of us are happier since we made the decision.'

My Reflection
While partners can often accept differences between them, it can be harder when children are involved, because of the level of responsibility both people feel for the children, and the challenge to their identity of not parenting their children in a way that is congruent with their beliefs and values.

In Solomon and Jasmin's case their differences were rooted in beliefs and values around nature and nurture that neither wished to change. As two people who studied human systems and behaviour, they knew very well how different people could be, but they felt unable to talk together about their own fundamental differences.

For me, this became even more apparent when I saw them separately. Both talked about each other, and had a lot to say, and yet they had said very little of this to one another. Engaging is a key aspect of togethering, and their difficulty in talking to one another about their true feelings meant that they were unable to find consensus and agree on shared parenting or to agree to differ—they remained locked in a conflict that affected them and their children.

The deep anxiety that both felt in response to the other's parenting was relieved as soon as they accepted that they had approaches that could not be reconciled.

Sometimes, parting is a constructive solution to an unsolvable difficulty, and Jasmin and Solomon worked hard to find ways to part amicably, working together for their children. Bit by bit the initial heat and distress of their differences was diffused and they were able to talk constructively about the way forward.

Jasmin and Solomon came to understand that they were not better together and, while this took time and effort to accept, it was, in the end, the right outcome for both of them.

They developed a new, more structured relationship, focused around the wellbeing of their children and in which they worked well together, so that ultimately, in this way, they were better together. When I think about them I sometimes wonder if, just maybe, moments of communion might have re-entered their relationship.

Chapter Five

Reflections on Your Relationship

How are you? I'm aware the stories that preceded this chapter may have thrown up many thoughts, feelings, images, memories, sensations, questions, and considerations for you, regarding yourself and your own relationship, or relationships.

It's worth pausing here to think for a moment. If you reflect on the chapters and concepts in the twelve stories, what generated the greatest emotional response for you? That might be exactly what you need to know to ensure that you and your partner are in a relationship where you are able to say you have found the way to be better together, today and in the future.

My aim in this chapter is to remind you of some of the key themes of the book, and to ask you a series of questions that might help you to clarify your thoughts, hopes, and intentions going forward, and that may help you with any concerns you might currently have.

When answering the questions I suggest that you give an immediate *felt* response rather than a considered or thought-out one. This is because an initial feeling is the way into a situation, a way to find a possible opening; using the raw material that exists before our cognitive functioning calls upon our life experience to construct meaning. For example, someone startles us, and we think we are being attacked because this has happened to us in the past. We lash out, but then we realise it's a friend playing a joke. To be startled was a raw reaction, but it was the meaning that we constructed that caused us to lash out, as opposed to any other possible reaction. So, what I hope you will respond with is that very first felt reaction. This is where we start from in the endeavour to break the often unhelpful pattern of meaning-making that has been established, so that we can more clearly locate the difficulties in a relationship.

If you believe that you know what is wrong with your relationship, then I would ask you to put that to one side for the moment, while you consider the questions. This will allow for the emergence of new possibilities, which you may or may not have been aware of.

The first thing I'd like to ask you to do is to think about your relationship on a scale from 0 to 10 and give it a number. Once you've thought about your own response, what do you think your partner would say in response to that question? Might they hold a different view? Of course, your partner might choose to answer the questions too, in which case that would be helpful, but if you are answering on your own then think about what you believe your partner might say.

Secondly, how much energy do you have for making changes in the relationship, also on scale of 0 to 10? I ask about energy because change does require energy, along with resolve. And again, what do you think your partner's answer would be? In my experience people are often surprised by one another's answers to either or both of these questions.

When there is a felt sense of positivity around the response to these two initial questions then it suggests that conditions are favourable for improvement. A sense of negativity doesn't mean that this isn't possible, but it does mean that the partners are not, at that moment in time, able to find the energy needed.

In chapter one I talked briefly about the five main pillars in life that make up our being in the world. Alongside our relationships these are our health, our spirituality, our interests, and whatever it is in life that brings us a feeling of security. These five areas constitute our personal world and all of them can interact and impact one another. They reveal our beliefs and values and it is these pillars, expressed through our unique expectations and actions—our striving—that are often at the root of relationship conflict.

For the next step in assessing where the difficulties in your relationship might lie, consider each of these five pillars, for yourself, for your partner and for the relationship. What do they mean for you? What do they represent? Where do you feel a sense of ease or unease? If there is pain, where does it lie, for either of you or for the relationship? Do you feel that one, or more than one, is in difficulty, or under threat? Might your partner see things in a similar way, or differently? And how do these areas impact the relationship that you have together?

Next, I would ask you to look at your relationship through the lens of what I call togethering, meaning what is actively lived by you and your partner through being together. It is the unique existence and living of the relationship and its striving.

The four main aspects of togethering are Being (the amount of time spent together), Doing (the amount of energy in the relationship), Engaging (the ways in which the partners interact) and Agreeing (the degree to which the partners agree on the way to live in terms of the five main pillars).

In answering the questions that follow, if you find it helpful, give a response between 0 and 10 for each one.

Consider *being* first. What was your relationship like back at the start when you first met? How is it now? What might it be like in the future? Often, things that were apparent at the start are still there. They can seem less important with the passing of time, but they can also be magnified, either in your view, or in actuality. And time can be particularly important at key times in life: at the start of a relationship, building careers, starting a family, home improvements, illnesses, and loss.

Next, consider *doing*. I asked earlier in the chapter about your energy for change in the relationship. This is essential, but it is also valuable to ask how much energy you have for your partner, and how much they might have for you. How much energy do you give to the relationship? Would your partner give a similar answer, or a very different one?

The third aspect of togethering is *engaging*, which includes both verbal and non-verbal communication. Thinking about the communication between you and your partner: how do you play together? How do you work together? How much time do you spend thinking about the relationship on your own as opposed to considering the relationship together with your partner? Do you change what you would like to say and, if so, what feeling drives that?

Now I would like to ask you about the approach you and your partner take towards communicating with one another. Are you predominantly relational, analytical, or behavioural?

Someone who is relational is person-centred, engaging around another person's feelings and experience and truth, thinking about the impact on each other in the here and now. This is a very present style of engaging. A very relational couple will talk about how they are in the moment and their process.

A person who is predominantly analytical will make sense of things by analysing them and putting them into a context, for instance by referring to a person's history or to family systems.

Lastly, someone whose approach is behavioural wants to create structure on which to base action. They may want frameworks and guidelines and plans and lists as a basis for action moving forward.

If partners have different approaches they can find communication with one another difficult. It would be helpful to think: which of these, predominantly, describe you? And which describe your partner?

Thinking about the language you use: what word do you use to describe a good relationship and what word do you use for one that is not so good? What words does your partner use? There might be a word such as respect, which often crops up and that gives you an indication of a potential issue in the relationship.

Following your responses to the questions already asked, which of these do you think you would need: a witness, a referee, a facilitator, or a mediator? A witness can be affirming for both partners when a conversation needs to take place. A referee can say, 'Hold on, you're not understanding each other because you're not hearing each other'. A facilitator helps you to say how you are feeling. And a mediator will say, 'What are you both able to settle on here, to help you reach an agreement?'

The answers you give here may help you towards another way of thinking about your relationship.

The final aspect of togethering to consider is *agreeing*, or consensus. How do you view the world together? Thinking back to the five main pillars for us as individuals, where do you differ from each other and which of these differences matter? It is natural to disagree, however it is you and your partner's feelings around the level of agreement and disagreement that is important. For example, some couples disagree over parenting skills and this in itself is not necessarily a problem: the conflict arises when they cannot find an approach or compromise with which they are both satisfied.

Again, your answers might differ from your partner's, or they might not. These things might well have changed over time, and in different ways, for each of you and for the relationship.

Often, comparison is a cause for concern in relationships. It is natural to compare and so it is important to address any difficult thoughts or feelings that might arise because they highlight an unmet desire. The unmet desire might just be one of wanting reassurance that the comparison is unhelpful, or it might highlight areas for potential change. It's worth thinking about how you view your relationship in comparison to those of other people. It's natural to compare our relationships to our parents, or our friends, or even to people we read or hear about. How do you see yours? What are the aspects that you feel good about and what are the ones that concern you?

After looking at togethering, it would be valuable to think about your relationship in terms of the three key areas of understanding, appreciation, and support. In therapy, it is almost always one or more of these three areas that partners will talk about when they first arrive. These three areas address what is done, or not done, what is valued, what is communicated, and the way we make sense of this.

What is your response to each of these three areas, for yourself, your partner, and your relationship? Do you feel understood? Appreciated? Supported? How do you think your partner feels in each of these three areas?

Having given so much thought to your relationship through the previous questions, I now suggest that we focus on your experience in relation to the two continuums of communion/alienation and ease/unease (or disturbance). In communion we can, momentarily, lose our sense of separateness, of being alone in the world, or cast out, experiencing instead a sense of togetherness whereby we think we are understood and feel safe and connected. At the other end of the scale is alienation—a strong sense of distance, lack of connection, thinking we are not understood and, as such, feeling unsafe. All the answers to the previous questions will now help you in thinking about this next set of questions.

Think about communion and bring such a moment to mind. What was the context of the moment? Focus in on the exact moment, try to relive it, and recall what moved you into the feeling of closeness—was it a word, a touch, a glance, shared laughter, or something else? Recall the feelings that were present at that moment.

Think now about what being able to have a moment of closeness like that meant to you. What might it say about you? What has prevented those moments from occurring more frequently?

Now think about alienation and bring such a moment to mind. What was the context of the moment? Focus in on the exact moment, try to relive it, and recall what moved you into the feeling of alienation. Recall the feelings that were present at that moment. Think now about what a moment of alienation like that meant to you—what might it say about you? What has enabled those moments to recur or increase in frequency?

Next, think about a period of time or a situation when you have felt most at ease in your relationship. What was the context of that time? Bring to mind the exact time and try to recall what moved you into the feeling of ease—was it a word, a touch, a glance, shared laughter or something else? Recall your feelings at the moment of ease. Think now about what being able to have a moment of ease like that meant to you— what might it say about you? What has prevented those moments from occurring more frequently?

Finally, think about a moment or a situation when you have felt most uneasy in the relationship. What was the context of that time? Bring to mind the exact time and try to recall what moved you into the feeling of unease. Recall your feelings at the moment of unease.

Think now about what being able to have a moment of unease like that meant for you—what might it say about you? What has enabled those moments to recur or increase in frequency?

In reviewing your answers, it's worth making sure of the following: Have you been able to identify an actual occasion—one that both you and your partner would be able to recall? It's crucial to have a base from which to start.

In thinking about context, make sure you take a big enough step back to include significant things that you might at first forget—for example, a bereavement, accident, illness, major change, major disappointment and, of course, the positives—graduation, promotion, new arrival, major achievement, major change.

Think about what that situation meant for you, the way in which it was either personally affirming or threatening.

As a result of focusing on these questions, you should start to understand not only the kind of situations that move your togethering into and out of balance, but also more about the meanings for both of you at those times and how your separate ways of being are either affirmed or threatened in the context of your being together. In other words, what are the key elements that can ensure that you are better together in your relationship?

At this point, you have given a great deal of thought to how you and your partner are and to your relationship. The challenge now is how to use this new understanding. I believe that in the same way we are always learning about ourselves we also need to constantly be learning about our relationships. It is a process of constantly striving to understand and resolve concerns in such a way that a balance is maintained, so that overall we perceive more experiences of communion and ease than those of alienation and disturbance. The intensity of our most important relationships requires us to ensure that the intensity of our engagement in them is both proportionate and appropriate. Often, the most unhelpful thinking, at times when relationships are struggling, is that the other partner should understand you, while the most helpful thinking is, 'What do we need to do together to ensure understanding?'

In this spirit, I favour a specific but very simple communication structure. Initially, it can feel awkward and uncomfortable to adopt, but as you both become familiar with it and see the positive impacts, that awkwardness and discomfort will be replaced with enthusiasm and confidence.

This style of engaging requires you to communicate by sharing information in three parts. Giving each other this information is about teaching each other about your differing ways of being, as opposed to justifying or explaining. Ultimately, it is about creating a relationship that most comfortably accommodates the people in it.

Communication Structure:
First, *identify* something that happened.
Agree together on the facts of the 'something'.

Second, say how you *felt*.
Consider your *thought response* and identify any thoughts that were about you.
Say why you think those thoughts come from those *feelings* and that situation.
Third, offer a *request*, something that you think will help you in future similar situations.
Now ask your partner to respond using the same format and talking about the same scenario, giving responses in the same way that you did.
Use this structure repeatedly (not necessarily at the same time; you might need to have a number of conversations) until you reach a level of understanding that enables you to settle on a request for each of you that can work for both of you.
Agree that any future requests and changes should be spoken about using this structure, to ensure that any changing situations are effectively integrated. As you build confidence through knowing that you can speak together about things that you have found difficult, you will be able to effectively ensure understanding and through that you will find ways forward. As this happens, the need for such conversations will diminish, but they will always be necessary because, as life and change happen, your relationship will need to adapt its togethering.
Let's bring this approach to life using an example.

Suppose you have noticed that whenever you and your partner talk about Christmas things do not go well. Bring the last time this happened to mind and think about exactly what happened. Are you able to pinpoint the disconnect through the differing words you both used? Maybe you identify that in the conversation your partner talked about what family members would feel and think while you wanted to plan the schedule of events.

Here's what you might say:

Identify something that happened: 'I notice that when we tried to talk about Christmas yesterday, we talked about it in different ways.' It is important to try to identify the point of disturbance or unease, so you might then say, 'I noticed that I wanted to talk about plans in terms of what would happen and when, while you wanted to speak about each of the family members' likely reactions and feelings'.

Say how you felt: 'When we have those conversations about Christmas, I end up feeling lost and bewildered because we never agree what we're actually going to do.'

Conveying the impact on you creates clarity and empathy. Now here's an example of the explanation you might give for your reaction: 'This makes sense for me because in the past when I wanted to talk with my parents about things that they found difficult they would always change the subject. I remember not knowing my alphabet before I went to primary school and worrying because I thought I should know it. When I asked my parents they changed the subject, and then when I went to school, I got very nervous and upset around spelling. If only they had helped me to prepare I'm sure I would have started school feeling more confident. I guess I like to know exactly what is going on over Christmas because then I think I will feel more confident and at ease going into it.

Now offer a request: 'In future can we have a meeting before the end of November to plan Christmas?'

Your partner might respond with something like:
Identify something that happened: 'Yes, I wanted to talk about family members' reactions and feelings, and I noticed you wanted to talk about plans.'

Say how you felt: 'When you wanted me to plan Christmas, I felt very anxious. I ended up thinking about how I can find myself in situations where something that was planned doesn't happen. I remember once planning my birthday party, I spent months thinking about who to invite, what the food would be and the games that would be played and then the day before my father got really drunk and was so horrible to my mother that she took us to our grandparents. My party was cancelled and I felt broken by the disappointment and the shame of having to tell my friends the party was cancelled.'

Now offer a request: 'Can I ask that we plan not to have a plan and then make time to talk to each other every day to ensure we are both okay? Could that be a plan?'

At this stage you are in very different places in terms of your request, but at the same time you both have clarity and a much deeper understanding of what is going on for the other. And this in itself can lead to empathy and to softening of stances and mutual agreement. A number of conversations along those lines might need to take place, but ultimately you might both agree, for instance, to have a loose and flexible plan, while also considering together how everyone coming for Christmas might feel or react.

When we have someone else to think about it helps us to let go of something in ourselves. And being heard and understood and supported can also generate confidence.

Whatever the final outcome, the important thing is that you both understand what is going on for the other. Reaching that place, sharing why certain things matter, what the meaning of them is for each of you, involves a depth of conversation that people don't normally have. And it allows you to look for possibilities for working together to resolve differences rather than taking rigid stances.

The hope is that in this way you can create a level of openness and trust, understanding what matters for each of you and each then being willing to make changes, individually and within the relationship, in order to be better together.

Last Word

This book has not been about what is wrong and right or good and bad in relationships, but rather a demonstration that relationships might best be understood, and therefore nurtured, developed, and repaired, through attending to how they are actually experienced.

Concerns within a relationship exist because the relationship exists. Both partners, not one, create the dynamic, which is why to blame a concern in a relationship on either partner is to miss the point. We are relational beings, and we impact and are impacted by our being in relation. And while partners undoubtedly experience their own truths, shared understanding is possible through the way in which they experience being in the relationship.

We might choose to see problems as being *ours* or *theirs*, but in practice they only get solved when both put that to one side and say *what is going on here and what can we do to change it?* And while psychological terms and concepts may serve to point the way, my experience tells me that they do not provide the solution in themselves and, at worst, they can be counterproductive as partners seek to defend themselves from being labelled with a diagnosis with which they feel uneasy.

For me, the focus for addressing our concerns when we get stuck is the question 'What is wrong *for* you (or me)?' and not 'What is wrong *with* you (or me)?' How do I know this? Well, next time you feel uncomfortable, see what difference using the question 'What is wrong *for* me?' makes, as opposed to 'What is wrong *with* me?'

This applies equally to relationship concerns, when partners disconnected or alienated from each other by pain, wonder: 'Is it you that is wrong, or me?' My experience shows that 'What is wrong for *us*?' is the best question to be asking.

Therapy is about getting to a limit of potential understanding and such a moment makes sense for me through the use of the word *epoche*. Other words people might use include revelation, a moment of pure being, authenticity. However, you might describe the experience as one of reaching the limit, letting go, a sense of being in a clearing and of there being a shift, new energy, possibility, and hope. I think of it as the point at which we stop thinking about what is wrong and instead come to *know* what is wrong for us.

Therapy doesn't end because a treatment has worked but because what needs treating has finally been fully understood and as such the process is the treatment. I am a facilitator of process, not a provider of treatment. Sometimes, I have a sense of what my client's existing process has yet to reveal to them and I might be able to do or say something to help, but most often it is my continued presence and faith in the process—theirs, mine, ours—that is most essential.

I have also realised that there are some experiences that have sustained my faith in the process of therapy. These are: firstly, witnessing how everyone has their own truth; and secondly, recognising that feelings are not to be judged, dismissed or denied, but understood. Disappointments and hurts that lead to further disappointments and hurts all serve to destroy trust in the possibility that a relationship can ever work. But often simply paying attention to what doesn't hurt and disappoint, can bring in just enough new energy to bring about positive change. This is revealed by the question 'What is right for us?'

The process that I am facilitating is the one by which we understand and make meaning in order to take action. Our feelings, including our bodily sensations, are a raw source of information that we make sense of by referencing previous experience and formulating or articulating it all through thoughts and language. Our relationship's conflicts and concerns arise because our process has not enabled us to fully understand and make meaning such that we respond optimally.

I work within a framework that recognises that individuals and relationships have their own unique ways of being in the world. Individually, we all understand and make sense of the world through our own unique process, with focus centred around our attempts to strive to be the best we can be in life. And I think of how our striving can be seen through the lens of the five main pillars that make up our personal world, our health, spirituality, our interests, relationships, and what brings us security. How we are in each of these areas will vary and be important in understanding ourselves along with what we bring into relationships to co-create its specific and unique dynamic.

In our relationships we need to share our process and work together on the tools through which we can understand and make meaning, in order to have a relationship that works for each of us. The framework I apply considers what it is like for each partner *to be* in terms of their levels of ease or unease in the four areas of togethering: being, doing, engaging, and agreeing. It is the unique ways of being of the partners individually that creates balance or imbalance. They are the areas of dynamic *happening* that will produce the overall sense of how the relationship is working and the partners' experiences of ease or unease, communion or alienation.

The last part of the framework is *my* experience of being in relation to the partners together and individually: the togethering that occurs during our time in therapy. Hearing the stories that partners bring, I am able to reflect on how I am impacted and how that might be helpful. I can often spot an external factor that may be a source of disturbance, and the way I am impacted can draw attention to how they impact each other.

All areas of the framework are essential, but I tend to find that most time and energy needs to go into considering the partners' engaging: either because is the core area of disturbance or because it has not supported the relationship in keeping its sense of ease in the other aspects of their togethering.

In our relationships we are at our best and better together when our experiences of ease and communion exceed those of unease and alienation, and this is possible when we are able to work together to answer the question 'What is right and wrong *for us?*'